The Institute of Chartered Financial Analysts
Continuing Education Series

Real Estate: Valuation Techniques and Portfolio Management

Chicago, Illinois
October 25, 1988

Barbara R. Cambon
Jeffrey D. Fisher
Susan Hudson-Wilson, CFA
Denis S. Karnosky
John S. Lillard

John L. Maginn, CFA
David L. McMillan
Michael T. Oliver, CFA
William T. Phillips
Robert H. Zerbst

Edited by
Susan Hudson-Wilson, CFA

Sponsored by
The Institute of Chartered
Financial Analysts

Additional copies of this publication may be ordered from

Institute of Chartered Financial Analysts
P.O. Box 3668
Charlottesville, VA 22903
1-804-980-3647
or
Professional Book Distributors, Inc.
P.O. Box 100120
Roswell, GA 30077
1-800-848-0773

Katrina F. Sherrerd, *Managing Editor*
Susan S. Brennan, *Production Editor*
Ellen D. Goldlust, *Editorial Assistant*
Joni L. Tomal, *Editorial Assistant*
Diane B. Hamshar, *Administrative Assistant*

ISBN 0-935015-11-6

Printed in the United States of America

Table of Contents

Foreword

Real estate has received much attention in recent years as a possible complement to traditional financial assets in both individual and institutional portfolios. The diversification benefits of real estate have been well-documented. But many fiduciary investors have been slow to accept real estate as a viable portfolio asset. Because of the increasing interest in real estate, the timing of the ICFA-sponsored seminar *Real Estate: Valuation Techniques and Portfolio Management* was excellent. The seminar, held on October 25, 1988, in Chicago, focused on several key topic areas in the real estate investment arena, including valuation of real estate, management of the asset allocation decision, design of real estate portfolios, and measurement of performance. The program was organized by Darwin M. Bayston, CFA, Executive Vice President, and Susan D. Martin, CFA, Vice President—Education and Programs. These proceedings are the result of that program.

The real estate field is complex and varied, and investing in it demands considerable experience and specialized knowledge. The speakers at this seminar shared their expertise and insights on many aspects of the real estate industry. We wish to extend our sincere appreciation to John L. Maginn, CFA, Mutual of Omaha Insurance Company, who acted as seminar moderator, and to the seminar speakers: Barbara R. Cambon, Institutional Property Consultants, Inc.; Jeffrey D. Fisher, Indiana University School of Business; Susan Hudson-Wilson, CFA, John Hancock Properties, Inc.; Denis S. Karnosky, First Chicago Investment Advisors; John S. Lillard, JMB Institutional Realty Corporation; David L. McMillan, Frank Russell Company; Michael T. Oliver, PRA Real Estate Securities Advisors; William T. Phillips, Stanford University; and Robert H. Zerbst, Piedmont Realty Advisors.

Special thanks are extended to Susan Hudson-Wilson for editing these proceedings.

Katrina F. Sherrerd
Assistant Vice President
Research and Publications

BIOGRAPHIES OF SPEAKERS

Barbara R. Cambon is Principal of Institutional Property Consultants, Inc., where she works with pension clients in formulating and implementing long-term strategic investment plans for real estate. During her career with the firm, Ms. Cambon has had primary responsibility for real estate investment performance research, and directed the development of the firm's computerized Real Estate Performance Monitoring System. Ms. Cambon is a member and serves on the Board of Directors of the Pension Real Estate Association. In addition, she participates in the National Council of Real Estate Investment Fiduciaries and is a member of the Advisory Board of the National Real Estate Index. Ms. Cambon's work has been published in the *Journal of Portfolio Management*. She holds a B.S. from the University of Delaware and an M.B.A from Southern Methodist University.

Jeffrey D. Fisher is Director of the Center for Real Estate Studies and Associate Professor of Finance and Real Estate at the Indiana University School of Business. He served as Secretary Treasurer and member of the Board of Directors of the American Real Estate and Urban Economics Association (AREUEA), has been elected its 2nd Vice President for 1988, and will serve as its President in 1990. Dr. Fisher also is a member of the Editorial Board of the *AREUEA Journal*. He served as Chairman of the Real Estate Center Directors and Chairholders Association, and is a founding Trustee and Treasurer of The Appraisal Foundation. He is a member of the Curriculum Committee for the American Institute of Real Estate Appraisers. Dr. Fisher is a co-author of *Real Estate*, the forthcoming *Real Estate Finance*, and has published over 20 articles on real estate. Dr. Fisher holds a Ph.D. in Real Estate from Ohio State University.

Susan Hudson-Wilson, CFA is Vice President, Portfolio Management and Research, John Hancock Properties, Inc. Formerly, Ms. Hudson-Wilson was the Director of Real Estate Research and Regional Director-Real Estate Investments at UNUM Life. She is the author of three books on labor economics and investment analysis, and is a member of the Urban Land Institute, the American Real Estate and Urban Economics Association, the American Real Estate

Society, the American Economics Association, the Boston Security Analysts Society and the Financial Analysts Federation. Ms. Hudson-Wilson holds a B.A. from the University of Vermont and an M.B.A. from Boston University.

Denis S. Karnosky is Managing Director and Division Head of the Asset Allocation Division of First Chicago Investment Advisors, responsible for the development and management of asset allocation policy and strategy. He is a member of the firm's Investment Committee and Chairman of its Asset Allocation Committee. Previously, Dr. Karnosky was Deputy to the Undersecretary for Monetary Affairs and Director of the Office of Monetary Policy Analysis in the Treasury Department. He holds a B.A. from Blackburn College, an M.A. from the University of Missouri, and a Ph.D. from Duke University.

John S. Lillard is President of JMB Institutional Realty Corporation. Prior to joining the firm, Mr. Lillard was a General Partner of Scudder, Stevens & Clark, where he served as a member of the Board of Directors, a Director of Scudder Realty Advisors, and National Marketing Director. He is a Director of Cintas Corporation, the Mathers Fund, and Stryker Corporation. Mr. Lillard holds a B.A. from the University of Virginia and an M.B.A. from Xavier University.

John L. Maginn, CFA is Senior Executive Vice President, Chief Investment Officer, and Treasurer of Mutual of Omaha Insurance Company and United of Omaha Life Insurance Company. Prior to joining Mutual of Omaha, Mr. Maginn was associated with Continental Casualty Company (now CNA Financial Corporation). He is co-editor of *Managing Investment Portfolios* and *Managing Investment Portfolios: 1985-1986 Update*, and a contributing author of *The Determinants of Investment Portfolio Policy*. Mr. Maginn is a past member and former Chairman of the Board of Trustees of the Institute of Chartered Financial Analysts and a past member of the Institute's Council of Examiners and Candidate Curriculum Committee. He is a former Director of the Financial Analysts Federation and a past President of the Omaha-Lincoln Society of Financial

Analysts. He holds a B.S.B.A. from Creighton University and an M.S. from the University of Minnesota.

David L. McMillan is Vice President and Senior Research Analyst in the Real Estate Department of Frank Russell Company, where he directs the department's quantitative efforts. During his career with Frank Russell Company, Mr. McMillan has been active in developing performance measurement software and on-line access to performance data. He is also involved in quantitative research for clients. Previously, Mr. McMillan was a Systems Consultant at Arthur Andersen & Co. He holds a B.S. from Brigham Young University and an M.B.A. from Dartmouth College.

Michael T. Oliver, CFA is President and Co-Founder of PRA Securities Advisors, which invests in publicly traded real estate securities. Previously, he was associated with Kennedy Associates Real Estate Counsel, with JMB Institutional Realty, and with Alex Brown and Sons, where he was President of the Real Estate Analysts Group and the Real Estate Investment Trusts Analysts Group.

William T. Phillips is Associate Treasurer and Director of Real Estate Investments at Stanford University. Prior to assuming his current position, Mr. Phillips was Director and Senior Vice President of Pacific General. He is a trustee of KFF and Dodge & Cox Real Estate Funds, and a member of the Urban Land Institute and the Association of University Related Research Parks. Mr. Phillips holds a B.S. from the University of Colorado and an M.B.A. from the University of California at Berkeley.

Robert H. Zerbst is President of Piedmont Realty Advisors. He is a member of the Board of Directors of the American Real Estate and Urban Economics Association, and serves on the Advisory Boards of *The Journal of Portfolio Management* and *The Appraisal Journal*. He is also a member of the American Society of Real Estate Counselors, the American Institute of Real Estate Appraisers, the Urban Land Institute, and the Pension Real Estate Association. Dr. Zerbst holds a B.A. from Miami University, and an M.A., an M.B.A., and a Ph.D. from Ohio State University.

Overview of the Seminar

Katrina F. Sherrerd

The importance of real estate as an asset class in investment portfolios has grown considerably in recent years. Real estate is attractive to investors because of its return potential and diversification benefits. Since 1970, the mean annual return to real estate has been 10.7 percent, with a standard deviation of 2.3 percent. Over the same period, the return to U.S. equities was 12.3 percent and the standard deviation was 19.9 percent. In addition, statistical analysis shows that real estate is a good portfolio diversifier; composite returns on real estate have low and sometimes even negative correlations with all types of stocks and bonds, and high correlations with U.S. Treasury bills and inflation.

Historically, the real estate industry was dominated by investors searching for the best individual property to acquire, without regard for the interrelation between properties and locations. Increasingly, the industry is moving toward an appreciation for the dynamics of portfolios and so is seeking properties to complement the goals and constraints articulated for the overall portfolio. As the role of the asset class grows, so will the importance of more exhaustive and accurate portfolio analytics.

There are many reasons why real estate is growing in importance within the investment industry. First, the unique risk-return characteristics and diversification benefits of real estate make this asset attractive to portfolio managers. Second, the liquidity of the real estate market is increasing. The market is becoming more liquid for two reasons: the number of players is growing and a large number of innovative vehicles such as CMOs and REITs are being developed and expanded. In addition, the market is becoming national in scope; no longer are projects dependent on local capital as the only source of funding. Finally, the real estate market is so large and so accessible that it demands the attention of portfolio managers. As Maginn notes in his opening remarks, the size of the commercial real estate market in the United States is estimated to have a market value in the mid-$3 trillion range; this is roughly comparable to the size of the U.S. common stock market.

As the real estate industry grows, the demands for higher quality information are building. Many difficult conceptual and practical issues require resolution. Valuations are not consistent, data is not readily available, and risk is hard to measure. The problems of real estate valuation include: infrequent trading, limited comparable property information because of the privacy of transactions, and the high cost of appraising individual properties. Because valuation is difficult in real estate, other aspects of real estate analysis such as performance measurement, risk analysis and management, asset allocation, and the comparison of real estate with other asset classes become difficult as well.

The data available in the real estate industry are largely idiosyncratic. There are problems with both the quality and the comparability of data, and the return data from current sources are not directly comparable to returns from other asset classes. This remains a problem for portfolio managers and real estate investors.

The measurement and analysis of real estate risk is key to the portfolio management concept. As a result of the serious problems in this area, the application of portfolio concepts to real estate has been impeded. The sophisticated analytical techniques used elsewhere in financial markets have not been applied to the real estate market to a significant degree. But the degree of rigor is rising rapidly, and analysis is becoming more similar to that of the other asset classes.

The presentations in these proceedings address the issues of concern to investors in the real estate market, including valuation of real estate assets, management of the asset allocation decision, design of real estate portfolios, managing risk in the real estate industry, and measurement of performance. In addition, the speakers examine the constraints and describe the newest techniques in valuing real estate and in portfolio management.

OPENING REMARKS

In the introduction to this seminar, John Maginn summarizes the critical issues facing investment professionals contemplating real estate investments. He reviews the characteristics of real estate that make it attractive to investment professionals and the problems that make investment in real estate a challenge. Maginn notes that real estate has long been considered something of a "distant cousin" in the investment profession, but that this image is beginning to change. He outlines several reasons why the real estate market demands our respect and attention, as well as some of the critical issues that remain in the industry.

Maginn notes that real estate is an investment that lends itself to the application of many of the valuation and portfolio managment principles that have been developed in the securities markets, but that many of these techniques have not yet been adopted in the real estate industry. The real estate market is characterized by complexities and inefficiencies that affect the availability, credibility, and breadth of data. But there is evidence that things are changing. Maginn feels that the investment rigor that is beginning to characterize the real estate industry will benefit everyone interested in investments.

OVERVIEW OF THE REAL ESTATE MARKET

In this presentation, John Lillard presents a comprehensive overview of the real estate market today and outlines some of the evolving trends, with emphasis on the impact of tax reform, foreign investors, and supply constraints.

Lillard discusses several reasons for investing in real estate, and several of the drawbacks. The advantages include: good diversification benefits, high risk-adjusted returns, low volatility, and protection against inflation. The drawbacks from investing in real estate include the fact that real estate is less marketable than securities, volatility is believed to be greater than the valuation methods imply, and the real estate market is less efficient than other security markets. Overall, from a portfolio perspective the benefits outweigh the drawbacks. Lillard illustrates the extent of the advantage with graphics.

The outlook for real estate investments varies depending on one's perspective. Lillard concludes with a few comments on the outlook for different segments of the real estate market over the next several years.

VALUATION OF REAL ESTATE

The factors affecting incentives for investing in real estate have changed quite a bit over the years. In this presentation, Jeffrey Fisher discusses how to value real estate investments in all environments. He notes that the valuation of real estate is an endeavor marked by many unanswered questions. Nevertheless, progress is being made.

Fisher begins with a review of the six key factors that create value for real estate. The most important factor is the demand for space by users. Real estate value is also affected by the cost and availablity of substitute space, rental income, demand for rental income, transferability of property rights, and the characteristics of the property that make it unique.

After considering how real estate value is created, Fisher discusses what value is being measured. There are numerous ways to conceive of the value in real estate, including market value, investment value, and appraisal value. He discusses the advantages of the most frequently encountered measures of real estate value.

The measurement of real estate risk is key to the portfolio concept. However, there are difficulties with measuring the risk of real estate assets because of the nature of real estate. After enumerating these difficulties, Fisher notes that real estate markets are not efficient in the sense that equity markets are. Because of this, fundamental analysis and research is valuable on the margin and on average in real estate, whereas it is probably not profitable on the margin in the stock market. Fisher draws several conclusions about investing in the real estate market: (1) information comes at a high price; (2) one needs to develop expertise to be successful in real estate; and (3) knowledgeable buyers can make money by taking advantage of market inefficiency.

Finally, Fisher describes three approaches to measuring value: the cost approach, the market approach, and the income approach. In theory, all three approaches would produce the same answer, but in reality they do not.

MEASUREMENT OF RISK IN REAL ESTATE

In this session, David McMillan discusses the attractiveness of real estate to portfolio managers and the problems of measuring the risk of real estate investments. McMillan cites three reasons that real estate is an appropriate investment for portfolios: (1) real estate represents the single largest store of wealth in the world; (2) real estate is a good inflation hedge; and (3) real estate provides portfolio diversification. McMillan concentrates on the diversification benefits of real estate in this presentation.

To determine the diversification value of real estate in portfolios, it is necessary to understand risk and return in the real estate market. Evaluating real estate as an asset class within a portfolio of assets is difficult because the meaurement of risk is problematic. In most cases, the standard deviation of return is used to measure risk. This measure does not apply as well to real estate as it does to equities. McMillan elaborates on the problems with using different risk measures for real estate. He suggests that Real Estate Investment Trusts (REITs) may be used as a proxy for the underlying real estate market that does not have some of the data problems that direct real estate investments have. He believes that comparable risk measures are more likely to be found in an actively-traded auction market for real estate securities than in an index of appraised values.

NONDIRECT REAL ESTATE INVESTMENTS

Because of the difficulties in measuring risk and comparing real estate with other asset classes, some people favor non-direct investments in real estate. In this session, Michael Oliver describes the advantages of investing in publicly traded real estate securities as an alternative to other equity real estate investments.

Oliver cites four reasons that portfolio managers should consider the inclusion of publicly traded real estate securities in their investment portfolios: (1) they are hybrid securities whose performance is similar to both stock equities and direct real estate ownership; (2) these securities should offer attractive opportunities to those who are able to commit resources to research the market; (3) these securities have many attractive characteristics; and (4) many of these securities sell at relatively high yields. Overall, Oliver believes that these securities are a prudent way to partake of the real estate business in addition to direct investing.

MANAGEMENT OF THE ASSET ALLOCATION DECISION

This two-part session addresses the problem of managing the asset allocation problem. In the first part, Denis Karnosky points out that investors are broadening their perspective on what constitutes an institutionally acceptable asset class. Increasingly, real estate is included in this view. In this context, optimal allocation within a portfolio becomes an important problem.

In this presentation, Karnosky reviews the risk-return characteristics and correlations of the assets that comprise the investable capital market. Based on the data since 1970, real estate is an important asset class. Karnosky also describes the results of research on whether portfolio managers add value through active stock selection or timing decisions. The results show that the dominant decision is the initial asset allocation decision: Timing and selection decisions reduced the average return on pension portfolios in the sample.

Karnosky concludes that real estate decisions must be made in a portfolio context, and must be integrated into the portfolio process. Failing to evaluate real estate investments from all perspectives will result in suboptimal management of what might otherwise be a very efficient, productive asset class.

In the second half of this session, Susan Hudson-Wilson discusses how important portfolio design is to the success of a real estate investment program. She notes that the concept of managing real estate investments as a portfolio is new to the real estate industry. It is an overdue concept which is now being developed because real estate is no longer considered a nontraditional investment area.

In Hudson-Wilson's opinion, research is the foundation for good investments in real estate: It should guide both individual investment decisions and design of portfolios. It is important to conduct objective research and to set standards which may be applied across different locations, properties, and time periods. The success of all research efforts depends on the quality of the underlying data. She elaborates on the type of research that is being done in the real estate industry, and the type that should be done. Historically, the real estate industry has not had a good statistic for evaluating the markets. To fill the void, John Hancock Properties created its own proxy for real estate returns. Hudson-Wilson describes this statistic, and shows how such information may be used to make real estate portfolio decisions.

DESIGN OF REAL ESTATE PORTFOLIOS

The design of real estate portfolios for institutional investors is based on one's underlying beliefs about real estate and real estate markets. In this presentation, Robert Zerbst presents his investment philosophy and describes how that philosophy affects the design of real estate portfolios, commenting on the use of various financial structures in the construction of real estate portfolios. In particular, he feels that real estate is a local product, that superior performance results from owner management, and that markets for well-located, fully-leased properties are overpriced. Against this backdrop, he presents alternatives for approaching real estate investments.

Zerbst describes two strategies for increasing returns in the real estate market: initiate the investment in earlier stages of the real estate life cycle or utilize financial structuring. Real estate projects may be categorized according to their stage in the investment life cycle. Zerbst reviews the investment risk and return profile associated with each of the four investment life cycle phases: (1) the raw land or predevelopment phase; (2) the construction phase; (3) the leasing phase; and (4) the operating phase.

Investment in the earlier phases of the investment life cycle involves assuming higher risks to achieve higher expected returns. The alternative is to use financial structuring to increase the return potential of an investment. Zerbst describes two financial structures that are being used in the industry: joint ventures and participating mortgages. The performance of these structures is a function of several factors discussed by Zerbst in this presentation. Zerbst outlines how these structures perform under alternative scenarios.

MANAGEMENT OF REAL ESTATE PORTFOLIOS

There are many techniques for managing real estate portfolios. In this session, William Phillips discusses the approach used at Stanford University. Stanford has allocated a relatively large portion of their endowment to real estate—approximately 16 percent. By most standards, this is an aggressive posture. According to Phillips, Stanford's relatively large allocation to real estate is a function of the University's investment philosophy for its endowment. That philosophy is based on the perception that educational institutions have some unique problems in terms of competitiveness and growth in the future. Stanford believes that it is critical for the University's performance and growth that the endowment achieves higher than average returns. Phillips describes how this philosophy has influenced their strategy for investing in real estate, and how the real estate portfolio has performed in recent years.

MEASUREMENT OF THE PERFORMANCE OF REAL ESTATE

In this session, Barbara Cambon discusses various measures that can be used to assess the performance of real estate investments. The methods traditionally used to measure the performance of financial instruments are not always appropriate for measuring the performance of real estate investments. Cambon notes three basic areas of difference between real estate investments and other investments: (1) the basic pricing mechanism is different; (2) the cash flow streams are different; and (3) the availability and timing of investments are different. These differences affect performance measures. Cambon provides examples of some simple formulas in this presentation.

Opening Remarks

John L. Maginn, CFA

With the exception of gold and precious artwork, no investment seems to generate as much emotion as real estate. Prime location, trophy-class property, glass palace—the language of real estate is rich with imagery that titillates the imagination of even the wiliest investor. Real estate is also an investment asset with characteristics that lend themselves to the application of many of the valuation and portfolio management principles that have been developed in the securities markets. Like securities in the 1970s, real estate in the 1980s has been the subject of increased academic scrutiny. The stream of articles in both academic and practitioner journals that relate portfolio management principles to real estate is evidence of this evolution.

Real estate has long been considered something of a "distant cousin" in the investment profession. Demystifying real estate and positioning it within the mainstream of investment rigor is the goal of these proceedings.

The real estate market demands our respect and attention for a variety of reasons. First, the size of the commercial real estate market in the United States is roughly comparable to that of the U.S. common stock market; both have an estimated market value in the mid-$3 trillion range. Worldwide, the value of commercial real estate exceeds the value of all stock markets.

Second, commercial real estate is a hybrid investment—it has both fixed-income and equity characteristics. Cash flows from lease revenues may be analyzed using both bond analysis techniques and risk-return valuation criteria, such as duration. In addition, options in leases, as well as the inflation hedge and appreciation characteristics of real estate, may be valued using generally accepted financial technology.

Third, the diversification and covariance benefits of real estate have been widely advertised and documented in many studies over the past 20 years. Recent studies, including data from the 1980s, reflect somewhat higher, albeit still statistically low, coefficients of correlation between commercial real estate and securities.

Fourth, relative differences in the liquidity of real estate investments and the volatility of published real estate return series raise questions about the accuracy and comprehensiveness of real estate values and valuation methods.

Fifth, questions have been raised about the lack of or limited scope of region- and property-specific risk-return sensitivity in the traditional real estate valuation models.

Sixth, an important aspect of a successful asset allocation model is the ability to redeploy assets and rebalance the portfolio as risk-return relations change with time. Real estate's liquidity or, some would say, illiquidity characteristics impose a constraint on the use of commercial real estate investments in an actively-managed, multiasset portfolio.

Seventh, I cannot help but analogize between the ascent to respectability that was afforded common stocks during the 1960s, and the current trend to institutionalize real estate. Both took place after a peak in the average annual return of the asset classes had been realized in the previous decade.

Eighth, the way that real estate investments are managed within the context of a portfolio of real estate investments today also seems a throwback to the securities markets of the 1960s. Real estate portfolios appear to be populated with good deals. Little consideration is given to the relation of the risk-return characteristics of each piece of property to the characteristics of the other holdings in the portfolio.

These proceedings have two objectives.. The first goal is to examine the newest and most effective techniques in valuing real estate. The premise is that the sophisticated, rigorous analytical techniques that have been developed for other classes of investments, such as bonds and stocks, are applicable to commercial real estate to a significant degree. Acceptance of these valuation techniques will add to the credibility of real estate as a *bona fide* investment alternative, and will also allow the determination of risk-adjusted returns for real estate investment. The second objective flows from the first: To the extent that reliable, historical expected risk and return data may be generated using these more rigorous and systematic valuation techniques, portfolio management theories and disciplines may be applied to the management of real estate portfolios, both as a single portfolio and also within the context of multiasset cash/bond/stock real estate portfolios that characterize the institutional segment of the investment business.

In the early 1980s, Professor Don Tuttle and I co-edited the first edition of *Managing Investment Portfolios*. It was the first practitioner-oriented book devoted to the subject of portfolio management, and it introduced real estate as a portfolio asset. Professor Jeffrey Fisher, whose presentation appears later in these proceedings, authored the real estate chapter and argued that real estate merited inclusion in multiasset portfolios. He also argued that the rigors of the portfolio management decision-making process, including valuation techniques, hedging and option strategies, and asset allocation models, were applicable to a broad range of investment alternatives, including real estate. In our current work on the second edition of *Managing Investment Portfolios*, the real estate section has undergone more comprehensive change than any other portion of the book, reflecting the evolution in real estate investment valuation and portfolio management techniques that is currently taking place.

I would like to make a few comments as a representative of the insurance industry, which has been a traditional investor in real estate. Insurance company investment managers have viewed with dismay and apprehension the influx of pension fund and foreign investors into the U.S. real estate markets. The effect of this influx on values has changed the game. Some insurance companies have joined the current quest for trophy properties and contributed to the two-tiered market and, some would opine, a glut of glass palaces in certain markets. Others have experienced the risks of loading up on "good deals" without sufficient regard to geographic diversification, particularly down in the oil patch. A few firms have taken advantage of current valuation levels to realize capital gains that far exceed the greediest of their expectations. It remains to be seen whether five years from now those opportunities will still appear as attractive as they do today.

The investment rigor that is beginning to characterize the real estate industry will benefit everyone interested in investments. The timing of these proceedings is particularly propitious. Capitalization rates for tier-one properties are at historically low levels on a relative basis. For security types, that is equivalent to historically high price/earnings ratios on common stocks. As mentioned earlier, annual returns on commercial real estate in the United States peaked in the late 1970s and early 1980s, and have since declined, most recently to the single-digit range. Tempered inflation trends and the muting, if not elimination, of tax advantages that favored real estate underlie the supply-demand trends in the commercial real estate market today. Too often, it seems, these trends are overshadowed by the triumphant announcement of a trophy property transaction at an astronomical price.

Significant strides have been made in systematizing the valuation process and developing more disciplined approaches to diversifying real estate portfolios since the Institute sponsored its first seminar on real estate in 1985. Significant problems exist, however. Real estate properties are not securities. The real estate market is characterized by complexities and inefficiencies that affect the availability, credibility, and breadth of data. These proceedings do not attempt to homogenize the markets, but to draw relations between the two that may be appropriate, and to suggest methods for utilizing valuation and portfolio management techniques that have evolved out of the capital asset pricing model, modern portfolio theory, and arbitrage pricing theories.

Overview of the Real Estate Market

John S. Lillard

Real estate is not a very complicated business. It is a business of supply and demand—a common-sense business. On a macro level, the process of examining individual properties that appear to perform very differently may be quite confusing. To be a successful real estate investor, one must view the business on a micro level—location, location, location.

Operating in the real estate capital markets before 1970 was a much simpler business than it is today. In that period, two sources of funds existed: mortgage lending and equity investing. The banks, thrifts, and insurance companies typically made straight 20- to 30-year fixed loans. The equity investors were principally the developers; they needed little additional capital prior to the late 1960s. There was also quite a bit of private syndication in the 1950s and 1960s, prior to public syndication.

Real estate markets began to change significantly around 1970. Beginning in this period, real estate was characterized by a great deal of volatility caused by inflation in the 1970s; disinflation in the 1980s; more integrated financing; shifting capital sources; and new investors, such as pension funds and foreign investors, who entered the market. In addition, demographics began to change. Urban clusters—small cities growing up outside the larger cities—began to grow, and the service economy began to develop. In this era, food service became very important, and malls sprang up everywhere, although the first enclosed mall was built in the early 1950s. In the 1970s, ownership began to shift from developers and users to investors. In the 1940s, properties were owned principally by developers, users, and, in cities like New York City, families who had been in the business for years. Real estate today is a very big market. By some estimates, the market for investment-grade real estate is $1.7 trillion. Real estate financing is much larger than both the bond and stock markets.

WHY INVEST IN REAL ESTATE?

There are several reasons for investing in real estate. It provides diversification, high risk-adjusted returns, low volatility, and protection against inflation. The case against real estate must also be considered. First, real estate is certainly less marketable than securities. In the past decade, however, it has become more marketable and valuation has become more precise as professional players entered the market. Because property costs are so high, diversification is possible only for large investors, unless investing takes place through a fund or a securitized approach. Second, there are less historical data available for real estate than there are for other securities. Third, volatility is believed to be greater than the valuation methods imply. Finally, real estate is less efficient than other asset markets.

Property valuations are an important aspect of real estate investment. The Appraisal Institute uses three appraisal approaches: (1) present value of all cash receipts, (2) replacement cost, and (3) comparable transactions. The most important of these is the present value of all projected cash receipts. In the late 1970s, use of this approach became widespread. Replacement costs and comparable transactions had been the traditional way of valuing real estate. Today, however, one would not consider trying to value a leased building without heavy dependence on the present value approach.

INFLATION

The value of a property changes as conditions in the environment change. A period of lower inflation accompanied by lower interest rates (and higher prices on bonds) produces a similar effect on leased real estate—i.e., lower capitalization rates. The cash flows and the residual values rise gradually under such conditions. Leases are typically structured with a pass-through of rising expenses to the tenant, Consumer Price Index (CPI) escalators on office buildings, and a percentage of sales on shopping centers. Therefore, a lower internal rate of return may be accepted under conditions of lower inflation, lower interest rates, and lower capitalization rates, and cash flows and projected terminal values will increase more rapidly during periods of rising inflation.

Real estate is the only asset that has a highly predictable change in the cash flow as a result of inflation. It does not work property by property, but it works for a portfolio. For example, if six malls around the country were owned, the trend of inflation and cash flow should be a close fit, even if a mall in Houston, for example, was not doing well because energy prices were falling and affecting consumer spending there. Because of the way this valuation technique works, there is very little volatility in the value of leased income property. This lack of volatility is often blamed on a sluggish valuation process. I think, however, that it is principally caused by the projected relation between leased income, terminal value, and inflation.

Real estate's stability is illustrated in Table 1. The differential between the high and the low real estate returns, under conditions ranging from deflation to rapid inflation, is less than for other asset classes. Figure 1 shows the returns for real estate, stocks, and bonds from 1971 to 1987. This shows how real estate has been relatively stable compared to stocks and bonds.

Many people think that inflation alone will affect the value of real estate. Figure 2 shows office occupancy levels and real estate returns for the past 15 years. Over this period, real estate appreciation correlates very well with office occupancy levels. By coincidence, the CPI would also correlate well with office occupancy levels during that time period. But a rising rate of inflation over the next two to three years will not fill empty buildings. Instead, inflation raises the cost of entry into the market, deterring development of new buildings until projected rents rise. As the buildings fill up and rents begin to rise, the values will move higher. Thus, the lag between inflation and its effect on property values may be significant.

FIGURE 1. Real Estate Lowers Portfolio Return Volatility

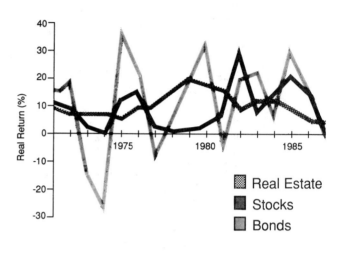

Sources: National Council of Real Estate Investment Fiduciaries, Frank Russell Company, Standard & Poor's Corporation, Shearson Lehman Bond Index

DIVERSIFICATION

The benefits of diversification into real estate are illustrated in Figure 3. Over the 17-year period, it would have been possible to increase returns and lower annual standard deviation by moving from a portfolio that was 60 percent stocks, 40 percent bonds, and no real estate to one that incorporates real estate. Figure 4 shows that for the entire 17-year period, real estate did better than both stocks and

TABLE 1. Real Annual Returns on Assets Under Varying Economic Environments

Economic Environment	Real Estate	Precious Metals	Short-Term Investments	Bonds	Equities
Deflation	-2.5%	-8.0%	+10.0%	+10.5%	-4.0%
Price Stability	+3.5	-1.0	+2.2	+5.0	+13.0
Moderate Inflation	+4.5	NA	+3.0	+1.0	+10.0
Rapid Inflation	+6.5	+6.0	-5.0	-7.0	+4.0
Differential Hi/Lo	9.0%	14.0%	15.0%	17.5%	17.0%

Sources: Sprinkel & Ginetski; Morgan Stanley

FIGURE 2. 15 Years of Real Estate Appreciation versus Office Occupancy Levels

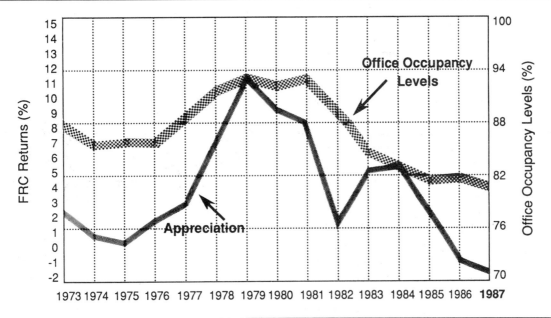

Sources: Building Owners and Managers Association International; FRC Property Index 1978-87; Frank Russell
Company Commingled fund data 1971-77

bonds, but that stocks and bonds have significantly outperformed real estate in recent years. The recent underperformance is largely the result of tremendous growth in the supply of property and the simultaneous decline in the rate of inflation. Under these conditions, real estate has lagged, and financial assets have soared. This situation will change from time to time, as it has in the past.

THE REAL ESTATE ENVIRONMENT

Figure 5 shows how key real estate variables—the relative vacancy rates, legislative mood, construction levels, and rents—change through a real estate cycle. We are probably in the third phase of the real estate cycle now. Typically, the cycle lasts five to eight years, but it varies from city to city, and even from

FIGURE 3. An Illustration of the Benefits of Diversifying into Real Estate for the 17 Years Ended December 31, 1987

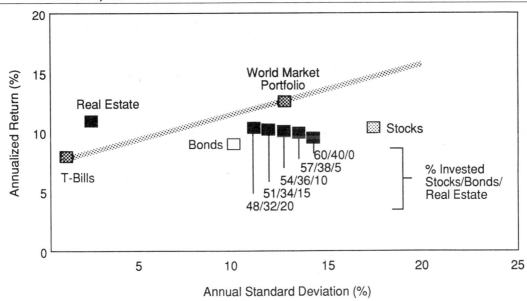

Source: First Chicago Investment Advisors

FIGURE 4. Property versus Financial Assets

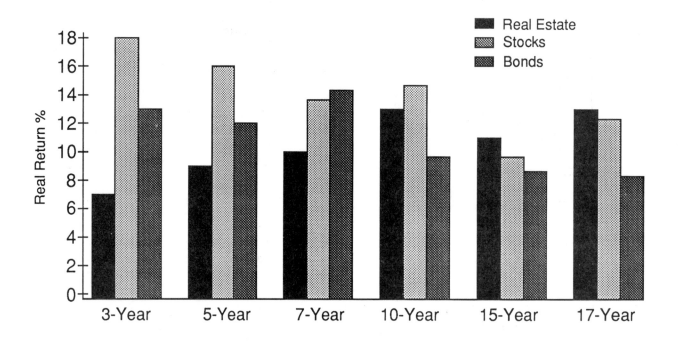

Source: National Council of Real Estate Investment Fiduciaries, Frank Russell Company, Standard & Poor's Corporation, Shearson Lehman Bond Index

FIGURE 5. The Real Estate Cycle

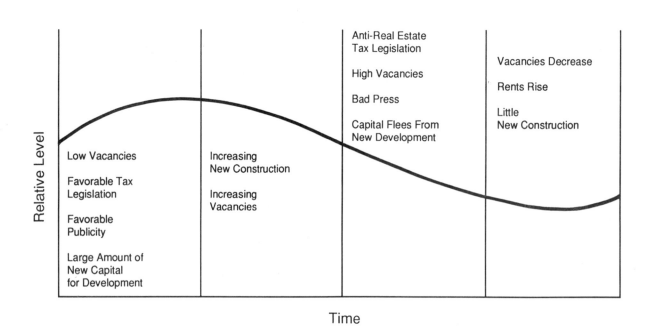

Source: Financial Strategies

FIGURE 6. Tax Rates Are at the Lowest Level in 50 Years

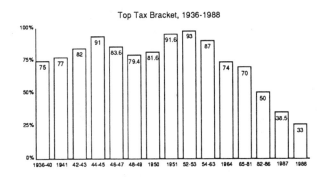

Top Tax Bracket, 1936-1988

Source: Grant's Interest Rate Observer

corner to corner. Certainly some cities are down in the fourth frame of Figure 5 already.

RECENT DEVELOPMENTS: CHANGES IN THE TAX ENVIRONMENT

The tax environment affects real estate values in many ways. In 1986, Congress passed the Tax Reform Act that eliminated many deductions and lowered tax rates. This reform has had, and will continue to have, a remarkable impact on real estate. Figure 6 shows that over the past 50 years, the highest tax bracket has always been considerably higher than the current rate of 33 percent. Many buildings being completed today were planned and started before the 1986 Tax Reform Act became effective. It may be another two or three years before the full impact of the new tax law is apparent.

The lower tax rates reduced the relative attractiveness of real estate to taxable investors. Table 2 shows internal rate of return estimates for four investor profiles on a specific investment proposal. A taxable investor under the old law in a 40 percent tax bracket—not the top bracket, which was 50 percent—could earn a 19.8 percent after-tax internal rate of return using 71 percent leverage on this particular deal. Under the new tax law, the same investor would show an 11.9 percent return. A tax-exempt investor, using the same amount of leverage, would earn a 17 percent internal rate of return on that same property under either tax scenario. In short, the tax-exempt investor went from being at a disadvantage under the old tax law to having a significant advantage over the taxpayer under the new tax law. Until the new tax law became effective, more than half of the return to most taxable investors came from tax benefits, rather than economic value, on most real estate transactions.

The Tax Reform Act of 1986 will have a significant impact on real estate markets. Many of the changes—for example, the higher capital gains rate (28 percent), lower ordinary tax rates, longer depreciation periods, changes in the at-risk provision, and changes in the way losses can be written off against other income—directly affect real estate return calculations. These changes are very significant and remove what has been in the past a tax subsidy for commercial property. If the present tax rates are allowed to stand, rents across the country should begin to increase when the current glut of supply is worked off, because the subsidization of construction that has existed for so many years will no longer exist.

TABLE 2. Projected Internal Rate of Return After Taxes

	After Tax	Leverage	Tax Rate
Taxable Investor—Old Law	19.8%	71%	40%
Taxable Investor—1986 Tax Act	11.9%	71%	28%[*]
Tax-Exempt Investor—Leveraged	17.0%	71%	-0-
Tax-Exempt Investor—Free & Clear	13.6%	0%	-0-

*Assumes investor has no passive income to shelter.

Source: JMB Institutional Realty Corporation

FIGURE 7. Office Construction Rates (1971=100)

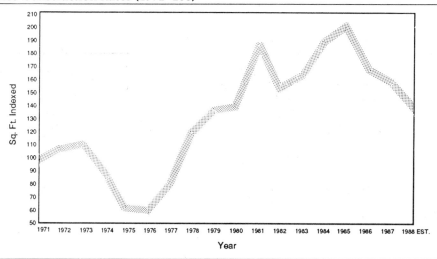

Source: Salomon Brothers

RECENT DEVELOPMENTS: SUPPLY CONSTRAINTS AND LEGISLATION

Recent developments in the real estate industry have an impact on supply. Construction has been declining in many markets, the syndication business has dropped off dramatically, and product orientation has shifted from tax-advantaged partnerships to income-oriented partnerships or real estate investment trusts (REITs). Foreign investors are very active in the market today. Prices are increasing and yields declining, similar to trends in the financial markets, as real estate valuations have become increasingly integrated with other markets here and abroad.

Figure 7 illustrates the trend in office construction rates from 1971 through 1988. The straight line represents an estimate of the amount of space that was absorbed annually. In the mid- to late-1970s, far too little space was built. Since the late 1970s, far too much space has been built—four times the amount absorbed during the past decade. Supply and demand are closer to equilibrium now, but construction will have to decline further to recover balance on a national level. This is a bad period in which to be a developer, but there are lots of developers out there, and many construction lenders are willing to give them money.

Supply constraints are increasing nationwide. People are voicing their concern about overbuilding, and they are getting more of a response politically than they were a few years ago. San Francisco is a good example. The people in Los Angeles rave about

the growth they have had in recent years, but the general reaction in San Francisco is, "Let them have it." In 1982, the public began to discuss restrictions on construction. Developers then rushed to build on every possible site, to beat the deadlines. Then, in 1985 and 1986, legislation was passed that effectively cut back office development to approximately 475,000 square feet per year for the entire city, provided the city liked the plans. No building met the city's criteria in 1986, so no new structures were built. Table 3 shows the statistics on the office market in downtown San Francisco over this period. Vacancy rates started at less than 1 percent in 1982, built up to between 6 and 10 percent in the 1983-84 period, increased to between 11 and 18 percent in the 1985-86 period, and have been declining since then, because there is very little new construction. We think the vacancy rates may decrease to as low as 3 percent by 1991-92 in the financial district north of Market Street. They would decrease even further if no change in rent occurred, but realistically, rents will increase so much that companies will move a lot of workers out of San Francisco. Rents averaged $35 to $45 per square foot in 1982 (high-rise buildings with a view of the Bay occasionally went for as much as $50 per square foot), and then declined so much that some major leases were signed at around $20 per square foot in top-flight buildings in the 1985-86 period. Rents are now $25 to $30 per square foot in the best buildings and rising. Table 3 also shows how the supply has changed and how demand absorption has continued fairly steadily at approximately 1.7 million square feet per year—this is more than 3.5 times the amount of new supply now permitted by law.

TABLE 3. San Francisco Office Market (Financial District)

	1982	1983-84	1985-86	1987-88	1991-92
Legislative Background	Public Begins Discussing Restrictions on Construction	Developers Rush to Build and Beat Deadlines	Downtown Plan: Construction Limited to 950,000 sq.ft./yr. for 3 Years	Further Permanent Limitation in Proposition M to 475,000 sq.ft./yr. for Entire City	
Downtown Vacancy Rates	Less than 1%	Building to 6-10%	11-18%	14% (late '87) 9% (late '88)	3%
Rental Rates Class A Building	$35-50/sq.ft.	$25-40/sq.ft.	$20-25/sq.ft.	$25-30/sq.ft.	
Demand Absorption	1,727,000 sq.ft./year on Average (mid-'70s through mid-'80s)				
Supply	23,465,000 sq.ft.	+7,150,000 sq.ft. (+3,175,000 sq.ft. sublease added)	+4,700,000 sq.ft.	500,000 sq.ft./yr. Average	

Sources: JMB Realty and Coldwell Banker

FOREIGN INVESTMENT IN U.S. REAL ESTATE

Foreign investors are playing a bigger role in the U.S. real estate market. Figure 8 shows that the United Kingdom owns the most U.S. property, almost $80 billion, followed by the Netherlands and Japan. The Japanese own about $35 billion worth of property. Most observers estimate that pension funds own around $60 billion worth of property, an increase of about $9 billion already this year. If the amount held by pension funds continues to increase at that rate, in three to five years, they would own more U.S. real estate than the United Kingdom.

The fact that foreigners invest in U.S. real estate shows confidence that there is value in this market, which is a reflection of the relative currencies and the trade surplus; foreigners must put those dollars somewhere. In addition, for the Japanese, the prices and yields on transactions in the United States are incredibly attractive. Land in Tokyo's central business district has sold for as high as $2 billion per acre. In the less attractive Ginza district, trades have taken place at $870 million per acre. That is a pretty high price for land, and it is reflected in the rents. Office space in the business district rents for $176 per square foot—the highest office rent in the world. Japan also has a very high capital gains tax rate on real estate (none on stock sales), so it is no wonder that properties are rarely traded. When they are traded, however, the current cash yield is 1 to 3 percent, compared to 5 to 8 percent or higher in the United States, depending on the quality and location of the building. That is a significant difference and certainly explains why the Japanese want to buy the best buildings in the United States.

Historically, the Japanese have been long-term investors, preferring trouble-free investments. Until recently, their purchases were concentrated on the east and west coasts. Now, it is estimated that 15 percent of the money they have invested in the United States this year is going into Chicago. Office space has been their principal area of interest; industrial property and hotels have followed close behind. The Japanese have not been very interested in retail property, because it is not managed in the same way in the United States as it is in Japan. Some of the larger companies want to buy raw land and develop it. The Japanese would like to do everything themselves, but they have hired U.S. managers when they are learning a business.

Several factors might cause foreigners to stop

FIGURE 8. Largest Foreign Investors in U.S. Real Estate (6/30/88)

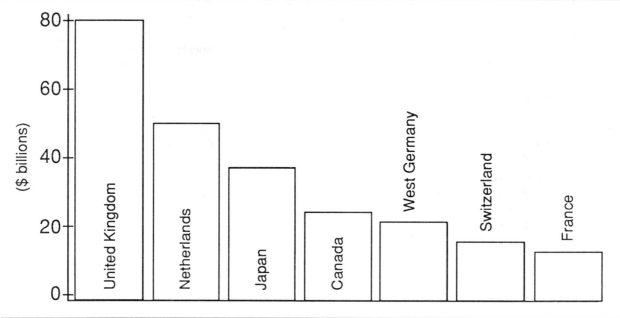

Source: International Real Estate Institute, Scottsdale, AZ

investing in the United States. These include a loss of confidence in the United States, a sharp rise in the price of oil, and the chronic inability to get the trade deficit under control.

THE OUTLOOK FOR REAL ESTATE

The outlook for the real estate business varies depending on one's perspective. Developers, builders, architects, and brokers should be concerned about the increase in legislative pressures at local levels and the tremendous oversupply that exists in most markets. Chances are that for developers, builders, and architects, in particular, business may not be good. Brokers, however, may continue to see a lot of transactions. For tenants, things could not be better in office, retail, and industrial properties.

Retail properties, such as malls, have been the darlings of the investment community. People thought that malls had a franchise—a built-in resistance to competition—because the "anchor stores" would not compete with themselves as a result of their operating covenants and their reluctance to expand geographically. The market would not support two similar malls in the same area. There are signs that this situation has begun to change. Several retailers now speak boldly about their plans to build a lot of stores over the next decade, even though they have taken on a tremendous debt. In a few cases, a developer has

assembled land and built a two- or three-anchor mall competing with a large mall that was already in place across the street. That is a new phenomenon. It is working well at Tyson's Corner, outside of Washington D.C., and many investors are watching to see whether it will work or be overdone in other locations.

The real estate market must be divided into segments to be analyzed at all. Even the difference between downtown office buildings and suburban office buildings is important to recognize. The vacancy rate for downtown office space in the United States is 17 percent: The vacancy rate in the suburbs is 26 percent. Although the national average for suburban office space is 26 percent, many areas have vacancy rates of 30 percent or higher, but several urban markets are in good balance. Strip shopping centers may be easily built, but have a minimal franchise to keep them from facing other competition up and down the street when a developer comes along and builds a better building. This vulnerability affects vacancy rates and profitability.

Some segments of the market have lower vacancy rates. Vacancy rates for industrial properties are lower in most locations. Industrial properties are quickly and easily built, but many industrial buildings are located in "in-fill" locations, where more space cannot be built. Many apartment markets have less than a 5 percent vacancy rate. Pension funds shunned these investments a few years ago, but now many of them recognize that they offer a real opportunity. Apartment buildings received preferred tax treatment under the old law; recently, the traditional financing of apartments has dried up. Hotels have typically been a disappointing business for owner/investors, though not for operators. In recent months, however, hotels such as the Plaza in New York have been purchased at extraordinary prices.

Other, longer-term factors will affect the real estate market. A burgeoning opportunity has developed as U.S. corporations restructure, take on debt, and sell real estate, which comprises 25 percent of corporate assets, and is often underutilized.

Demographics and the evolution of lifestyles will bring change. Apartments have long been occupied by population groups that are not growing. For example, by the year 2000, there will be 10 million fewer people between the ages of 18 and 34. On the other hand, the number of senior citizens will be much larger. Many people in these age groups consider apartments an attractive option, one in which somebody else takes care of the lawn. Thus, apartments are in many cases upscale residential-living approaches that are very popular with elderly people as well as with young professional couples.

The redevelopment of central business districts, which lagged for a long time, is now taking place with a great deal of momentum. Another factor to watch is the environment, in terms of legislation and its effect on real estate. People around the world are becoming more concerned about the environment: this growing concern will have a significant effect on real estate.

Question and Answer Session

QUESTION: Was your firm's decision to buy property in San Francisco based on a long-term view of rents in that area?

LILLARD: Yes, it was based on a long-term view of the rents—a three- to four-year view, actually. Typically, one will pay a higher price for something like that, but we believe the return will be very good because of the tightness of supply. We plan to hold the property for 10 or more years, and possibly even longer than that. Over that period, the cash flows should rise substantially as leases roll over to higher and higher rents.

QUESTION: Could you apply that analysis to other markets, for example, Houston, Atlanta, or Washington D.C.?

LILLARD: Yes, this type of analysis may be applied to all three areas. In Washington, there is an area not to far from the White House—the Golden Triangle area—that is very tight. Traditionally, Atlanta has been a very overbuilt market; there are too few constraints on supply. They managed to squeak by for a period of time because of the tremendous growth. Downtown Houston will become more attractive as a result of the lack of new supply; they stopped building downtown two to three years ago. Some buildings have traded hands at prices below construction cost, and when that happens, the new owner can charge lower rents than the previous owners. In these situations, developers have a hard time getting construction loans, because they cannot demonstrate that the rents will justify the cost. So downtown Houston will be coming back into balance, probably over the next two to three years. Many of the buildings will have to be altered to suit the clients in the suburbs, however. Houston has never had any zoning. As a consequence, if all of the suburban office buildings fill up with workers, there will be a traffic gridlock in Houston beyond imagination.

QUESTION: Please comment on the Denver real estate market.

LILLARD: Denver is very overbuilt. They will probably have problems for several years.

QUESTION: Please comment on the differences in the price trends between Class A, or trophy-type properties, and second-tier properties.

LILLARD: There are favorable transactions taking place every week, in both the trophy properties and second-tier properties. The Class A properties will typically hold their value better throughout the cycle. Often these properties are purchased by foreign investors who do not care about price, but are willing to wait until the deal can be put together. Typically, U.S. investors are more price-sensitive, but are willing to make a decision faster. Some buildings are not listed with a broker. In some cases, a seller will deal directly with another real estate player who is known to be an appropriate buyer. Turnarounds are tempting, but they are as difficult to pull off in real estate as they are in the stock market.

QUESTION: Are there indications of price weakness in the second tier?

LILLARD: Yes, in places like Denver, Dallas, and Atlanta, properties occasionally trade at lower prices. Many other markets are not showing any price weakness. For example, Washington D.C. is a high-priced market. It has been a very strong market in recent years, and even with the oversupply that is coming several blocks from the Golden Triangle area, one still does not hear about distressed property prices. Certain cities, such as Hartford and Philadelphia, have had a tight office market down- town and will experience high vacancy rates in 18 to 24 months.

QUESTION: What is your typical holding period for a property?

LILLARD: We have held properties for an average of six to seven years for our tax-paying investors, who still represent about 75 percent of all the property our firm has bought over the years. The holding period used to be principally a function of the tax benefits for many owners. Typically, it took seven years to run through most of the tax benefits and then a taxpaying investor could take a capital gain at a lower rate and move on. That situation no longer exists. We intend to hold properties for a longer period of time for tax-exempt investors—at least eight to ten years for apartments, and as long as ten to fifteen years for office, mall, and industrial properties.

Valuation of Real Estate

Jeffrey D. Fisher

Between 1981 and 1986, the three most important things in real estate changed from "location, location, location" to "tax shelter, tax shelter, tax shelter." Now, however, the answer may be "yen, yen, yen." I do not know what the adage will be in the next few years. Certainly, the factors affecting incentives for investing in real estate have changed quite a bit recently. In this presentation, I will discuss how to value real estate investments—no matter what the environment.

WHAT CREATES VALUE?

Before discussing valuation methods for real estate, it is necessary to review the six factors that affect the value of real estate. First, the key to the economic value of any property is the demand for space by users. This fact was almost forgotten between 1981 and 1986, when investments had after-tax rates of return that made sense, even when before-tax rates of return were not positive. The Economic Recovery Tax Act in 1986 eliminated many of the tax benefits of real estate, resulting in a renewed interest in the economics of the property.

Second, real estate value is affected by the cost and availability of substitute space—the supply side. This consideration must include both current and proposed space, as well as space that is being converted from other uses. One wonders why buildings are still being constructed in Dallas and Houston; there must be enough space available in those locations to meet needs for the next five to ten years. One explanation for this phenomenon is that many developers are afraid that if they do not undertake the project, somebody else will. Developers want to retain control of the good locations and to keep their workforce employed, because it is very expensive to lay off employees and then rehire them several years later.

Third, real estate value is a function of the rental income available from the space, which is in turn a function of the supply and demand for space. This value comprises explicit rent paid by lessees and implicit rent paid by users who both use and own the space. Rent savings may be a consideration in a user-owner's decision to purchase space. The tax law changes have had a great impact on whether corporations decide to own or lease space. From 1981 to 1986, many corporations engaged in sale lease-backs. During that period, it was often better for syndications and individual investors in high tax brackets to own the real estate and lease it to corporations, because corporations could not benefit from the tax structure as much as individuals could. With the passive-activity loss limitations under the new tax law, the advantages of ownership by individuals and syndications are significantly less. Corporations are still exposed to double taxation, but they may use the losses from real estate to offset other corporate income; futhermore, the highest corporate tax rate is now greater than the highest individual tax rate, which makes depreciation deductions more valuable to corporations. Thus, incentives for corporations to own real estate have changed; they are not necessarily at a disadvantage now.

Fourth, the value of real estate is a function of the demand for rental income by lenders and investors, which is derived from the demand for space. Investors are interested in the characteristics of the rental income derived from a real estate investment. The net operating income from the property is split between the debt and the equity interest in the property. Of course, each of those interests has different risk and return characteristics, and the structure of the debt determines the characteristics of that income flow. The nature of the lease terms, loan covenants, and even zoning requirements also affects the characteristics of the income stream.

Fifth, the transferability of property rights adds value to real estate. It is often said that real estate itself cannot be owned: real estate is the physical land and buildings—the purchase of a property is really only a transfer of property rights to the underlying real estate.

Finally, one should examine the characteristics of real estate that make it a unique investment. In general, real estate investments will be more attractive if they are in some sense unique and if they contribute to a diversified portfolio. One consideration is the way in which the income from real estate correlates with income from other investments. If the income streams are not correlated, some diversification benefits may be obtained from investing in real estate. Another consideration is the way that real estate income responds to unanticipated inflation. Presumably, all asset values reflect anticipated inflation, but they will not all respond the same way to unanticipated inflation. Historically, real estate has been a good inflation hedge.

WHAT "VALUE" IS BEING MEASURED?

After considering *how* real estate value is created, it is important to consider *what* value is being measured. Appraisers struggle with these issues constantly, and though appraisers are often criticized—in many cases rightly so—it is necessary to understand and appreciate the techniques that they use.

There are numerous ways of defining the value of real estate; I will outline six of them. In most cases, the most important value is the "market value"—the value of the property to a typical investor. Market value is supposed to be objective and independent of the specific investor. An alternate definition is that market value is the most probable selling price for the property. Market value is important for several reasons, one of which is that most appraisals require an estimate of the property's value to the next person who would purchase the property; this is not necessarily the same as the value to the person who last purchased it. The most probable selling price or resale price is a good way to think about market value for this purpose.

Many appraisers have argued that tax considerations should not be a factor in estimating the market value of real estate because market value is supposed to be independent of the specific investor. If the typical investor is tax-oriented, however, then tax considerations should be factored into the value of the real estate.

A second definition of real estate value is investment value; that is, the value of the property to either an individual or institutional investor. Investment value also takes into consideration the investor's current portfolio, diversification needs, and tax status. Thus, investment value may be quite different from market value. Some people joke that the term "investment value" is used when an individual value is too high to be called market value. The truth is, investors normally buy real estate when they think the investment value exceeds market value. Many people question why pension funds

bought real estate during the 1981-86 period, when real estate values appeared to be most attractive to tax-oriented investors because of the tax laws. For pension funds, the diversification benefits of adding real estate to a portfolio offset the fact that tax benefits could not be used, even though those benefits were implicitly included in the price. Under the new tax laws, it may make even more sense to add real estate to a portfolio; investors are probably not paying a premium for tax benefits now, so diversification benefits will be relatively greater.

Third, there is an assessed value of the property. Assessed value is supposed to be based on market value, but there are often limitations on how value is determined for property-tax purposes. Many of these constraints derive from state laws and legal decisions, which are sometimes inconsistent with valuation theory. Some states, for example, require the assessed value to be based on the cost approach to appraisal, which is only one of three possible approaches. Often, crude rules of thumb are used by the assessor to estimate value for assessment purposes.

Another value concept is the value of a property to a particular user—the value in use. This value may differ from market value, particularly on special-purpose properties, such as an industrial plant, that would probably not have much value in exchange but have high values to the current user. In these situations, the value-in-use concept is substituted for market value for property-tax purposes. For example, the John Hancock building may be far more valuable to the John Hancock Company than any cash price they could receive from selling the property, even if they were offered twice the building's market value and allowed to lease it back at a very favorable rate. Similarly, Sears may make a great deal of money by selling the Sears Tower, but will the company's image be harmed because they no longer own the Tower? A decline in the company's image could, in turn, affect the price of their stock.

Fifth, appraisers often must estimate the value of a proposed project. In these cases, they value the proposed project as if it were completed at the time of the appraisal, assuming current market conditions and stabilized rents. Of course, on a proposed project, those conditions will change before the project is completed. Thus, appraisers should consider three different values: (1) the value of the property prior to development; (2) the value of the proposed project after it is completed but before it is rented; and (3) the value of the property after the rent is stabilized. The value prior to development may in turn be based on a highest-and-best-use concept, which is the proposed use in the development plan. The value of the project after it is completed but before it is rented is not going to be the same as the value after the space is rented, because renting space takes time. Also, if the project was sold before it was fully rented, the marketing costs of renting the space would have to be included. If the project was sold as one large project rather than individual units, the value would have to be discounted. So, the value of the project at this stage is quite different from its value after the rent is stabilized.

Though hard to believe, some appraisers have reported the value after the project is completed and fully rented as the value the lender could use to establish the loan amount. In fact, lenders should only advance funds as value is created over time, from the value prior to development—in its vacant state—through completion and rent-up.

The last value concept is the going-concern value. This valuation method attempts to measure the intangible enhancement that a business provides to the value of land and buildings. The going-concern concept applies particularly well to malls, restaurants, and hotels. There are many instances in which a business is associated with the real estate. For example, a shopping center, especially a regional mall, is really a business. Thus, the value of the mall is a function of the value of the land, the building, and the businesses associated with that mall. In most malls, a big department store—Sears, for example—lends its trade name to the mall, signs a reciprocal easement agreement with the mall developer to share parking and common areas, and agrees to stay in the mall for a certain time. These business activities increase the value of a mall beyond merely the value of the land and buildings. Rents paid by smaller tenants in a mall include the right to use space, the benefit of associating with the other business activities in the mall, and the value of the advertising by the department stores and mall manager.

For these properties, it is difficult to determine how much of the total value is business value and how much is real estate value. It may be important to separate these values for property-tax and loan purposes. Property taxes should apply only to the land and buildings. Although most lenders determine the amount of a loan based on the collateral value of the real estate, others may not care whether the loan includes business value. The presence of a business does not necessarily make the investment more risky. It may, in fact, make the investment less risky because of the diversification benefits of investing in both real estate and a business.

REAL ESTATE MARKETS VS. EFFICIENT MARKETS

The risk-return characteristics of real estate markets versus efficient markets affect its valuation. First, it is difficult to measure the risk for real estate. Each parcel is unique; no two properties are exactly alike. This would not be the case in an efficient or perfect market. Because each parcel is unique—for example, different locations, lease characteristics, and so forth—it is difficult for an appraiser to base the value of a particular property on comparable sales of other properties. Questions always arise about the similarity of the comparable property to the property being appraised. For example, "Class A real estate" means different things to different people in different cities.

Second, real estate has a fixed location. The property is not transferable. Third, compared to more efficient markets, there are relatively few buyers and sellers in the real estate market at one time. Fourth, in an efficient market, buyers are supposed to be price-takers; this is not always true in the real estate market. Often, the highest bid for a property is much higher than the price the next person would have paid. This type of situation causes some people to question whether market value is really being paid for real estate. It has also been argued that there is an upward bias on the price of many real estate transactions because there is no short selling in real estate markets—pessimists cannot offset the optimists, as they do in the stock market.

Fifth, real estate is bought and sold in relatively large economic units that are not easily divisible. That is becoming less of a problem with securitizations, which attempt to make real estate more divisible by allowing the investor to buy an interest in an office building, for example, instead of requiring the investor to buy the entire building.

Sixth, the real estate market is not self-regulating, and includes many government controls. Environmental regulations, at the state level and perhaps at the federal level, may cause even more problems. Recently, members of my firm met with representatives of the Environmental Protection Agency (EPA) and of firms in the asbestos removal business to discuss more objective ways to measure the effects of asbestos removal on property values. The EPA is concerned that there are no standards by which to determine who should be in the asbestos removal business, or what it means to render a property free of asbestos. The EPA is considering putting a moratorium on the removal of asbestos until they can formulate better standards for how that process is monitored and who should be able to do asbestos removal. These environmental problems will probably result in more government regulations.

Seventh, supply adjusts very slowly in real estate; because of this, supply and demand are not always in balance.

Eighth, there is no organized or central market for real estate. Attempts are being made to provide better information about available properties, but as yet there is nothing like the New York Stock Exchange for real estate.

Ninth, information about product and market prices is poor in the real estate market. Buyers and sellers in real estate are not highly informed, which is probably the main reason it is so difficult to measure risk and return for real estate. It is not always clear what exactly is being bought. In some cases, the size of the building may even be uncertain. It has been said that every time a building changes hands in New York City, the building gets bigger. That is not because of renovation; buildings get bigger because of differences in the way space is measured. It is also difficult for a buyer to determine the amount of rent actually being paid when a building is bought. The appraiser will be told the nominal rent, but that figure does not include any tenant concessions. By the way, there is no longer such a thing as "free rent;" now, there is "early occupancy." When an appraiser asks how much free rent there is, buyers can say, "We don't give any free rent." One might be able to get into the building a year early, however. Thus, the real estate market is characterized by poor information about the product, the market price, and what is being sold.

Finally, the real estate market is characterized by infrequent trades of property rather than by continuous transactions. This is another reason why techniques used in analyzing stocks and bonds cannot be used to evaluate the riskiness of real estate. Continuous transactions are used to compute holding-period returns and for correlations between the returns on real estate and those of other investments. Without continuous transactions, those rates of return cannot be computed.

These considerations lead to several conclusions about the efficiency of real estate markets. First, information comes at a high price. Second, one must develop expertise to be successful in real estate investment. Third, knowledgeable buyers can make money by taking advantage of market inefficiency. It has been argued that fundamental analysis is profitable at the margin in real estate, whereas it is probably not profitable at the margin in the stock market. The average returns for fundamental analysis in the stock market may be high, but the marginal return will be very low. On the other hand, the marginal return on fundamental analysis in real estate is very high.

The real estate market is becoming more efficient as more sophisticated investors enter. Developers are finding ways to capitalize on the inefficiencies, making the market more efficient. The market is also becoming more national and international in scope. But the lack of information is still a problem. Pricing models that account for the years when a property does not trade would help. Such a pricing model might plot the value of real estate as a function of different market characteristics. The model would generate the prices a property should have sold for each year; it could be calibrated using actual sales of properties. Those intermediate sale prices, then, would be the basis for computing holding-period returns and for correlating the value of real estate investments with the value of other investments. Several efforts are currently underway to develop better risk-return models and databases that will enhance our understanding of real estate markets.[1]

APPROACHES TO MEASURING VALUE

Appraisers use three approaches to measuring the value of real estate: (1) the cost approach, (2) the market approach, and (3) the income approach. Because information is poor, the property and the market must be evaluated from several different perspectives, and the results of each approach must be compared to derive an estimate of the real estate's value.

The cost approach assumes that replacement cost is an upper limit on value and that the current use of the property is the highest and best use of the site. The problem with this approach is that the depreciation and entrepreneurial profit associated with the real estate are difficult to measure. Therefore, the cost approach is generally considered the least reliable approach to value.

The market approach is based on comparable sales. It assumes that value is based on the cost of properties with the same or comparable income potential, lease structure, expenses, risk, financing ability, property rights, and market conditions. The shortcomings of this approach arise because of the difficulty of finding properties that are truly comparable and because it requires recent sales of comparable properties. In addition, the price may include more than real estate, it may include the

---

[1] See Ms. Hudson-Wilson's presentation, pp. 42-49.

benefits of favorable financing or the value of a business as well. This approach uses only a small sample of the market—perhaps three or four comparable sales—as an indication of value. Further, because appraisers use sales that have taken place in the past, variations in the price of the property tend to be smoothed out. For that reason, market value is not a good basis for measuring the riskiness of real estate.

The income approach is based on the income potential of the property—typically measured as the present value of all cash receipts. Unfortunately, a number of appraisers take questionable shortcuts with the income approach. The income approach should rely on market information—rents, typical expenses, current and potential competition, changing demand, vacancy rates, and so forth. Often, though, appraisers use shortcut measures such as the overall capitalization rate—the net operating income of the property as a percentage of the sales price, which is analogous to a price/earnings ratio for stocks—that come from sales of comparable properties. This is really more of a market approach than an income approach, because it does not explicitly discount future income. Alternatively, an appraiser may use a capitalization rate calculated as the required discount rate on the property minus a growth rate. This shortcut is analogous to using a dividend growth model for stocks, but is still not appropriate for the analysis of most real estate investments.

It would be more appropriate to use a discounted cash flow analysis which is based on the present value of all cash receipts. Such an analysis explicitly considers income on a lease-by-lease basis, expenses, lease renewals, tenant improvements, and perhaps financing and tax issues. Appraisers consider discounted cash flow analysis a new technique, although many of the methods that appraisers have used in the past are actually based on a discounted cash flow analysis.

In theory, all three approaches to measuring value should produce the same answer. If an appraisal report produces the same number for all three methods, however, the appraiser should be viewed with suspicion, because the inefficiencies of the market will make it almost impossible to obtain the same answer from all three approaches. Using several approaches does provide a good cross-check on assumptions, however. Appraisers have gotten into trouble at times by not considering the effect on value of changes in the market, changes in the highest and best use of the site, or the absorption period for new properties. It is also difficult to value many of the options implicit in real estate deals, such as participations and rent guarantees. Few, if any, appraisers are familiar with option pricing theory, and, thus, they do not understand how to use the theory to value financing.

CONCLUSION

The valuation of real estate is an endeavor marked by many unanswered questions. What is market value? How do environmental hazards affect property value? Is the value of real estate being allocated to its proper components—real estate, personal property, and intangible business value? What is the appropriate risk measure for real estate? What risk is priced? How should real estate investors diversify—by location, by property type, or perhaps by lease type? How should real estate securities be valued? How should proposed projects be valued? How many sales constitute a market? Does financial leverage create value? Did tax reform affect real estate values?

Though such questions are troublesome as well as numerous, progress is being made toward answering the question of how to value real estate. Better analytical models are being developed that will enhance our understanding of the demand for real estate and of how real estate is priced. Several real estate centers around the country are currently working together to develop such models, and several industry organizations are collaborating to test some of these models. In addition, better databases for transactions are currently under development. There is also cooperation and consolidation among the major appraisal organizations. Uniform standards of appraisal practice have been developed, and an entity called The Appraisal Foundation has been set up by eight national appraisal organizations to provide for uniform standards and for uniformity among different states' certification requirements for appraisers. Finally, legislation has been introduced at the federal level that would regulate appraisers.

Question and Answer Session

QUESTION: Please comment on the difference between investment value and market value?

FISHER: Market value is the most probable sale price, whereas investment value is the value to a particular individual institution. Many people would like to say that what the Japanese are paying, what the syndications paid in the past, and perhaps what some institutional investors are currently paying, is really an investment value. I would argue that if these are typical investors, then they are paying market value. The problem is that people in real estate tend to think that values do not change much over time. There has been some reluctance to accept the fact that values in real estate do change, just as they change in the stock and bond markets. One must also accept that real estate is an international market; the price the Japanese are paying today is market value, even if they do not buy tomorrow.

QUESTION: Could one use the standard deviation of returns by region or by property type as a risk factor for real estate?

FISHER: If standard deviations could be measured by property type and by region, then that would be a basis for asset allocation on a geographic basis and on a property-type basis. The problem is that the data for measuring those standard deviations are not available.

QUESTION: With regard to the discounted cash flow technique, should one use one discount rate or should one use different rates for different cash flows?

FISHER: Theoretically, the different cash flows should be discounted at different rates if they have different risk characteristics. Perhaps the income from present leases on a property should be discounted at a different rate than projected income from lease renewals in the future, and the resale price of the property at an even higher rate. The problem, though, is that the appraiser must support the discount rate he or she uses in appraisals for market value, and it would be hard to justify objectively the different discount rates. For investment value purposes, different rates could be used, but this is probably not practical for market value estimates, where the market data are not available to support those different discount rates and where it is difficult to know how to measure those risk differences.

QUESTION: Should there be different discount rates for undeveloped land?

FISHER: The discount rates should reflect the riskiness of the investment. Undeveloped land or land based on a proposed project would normally be a riskier investment than an existing property that has been leased. A proposed project is subject to changes in supply and demand during the development period.

QUESTION: Don't all securitizations eventually trade at various discounts to market value?

FISHER: I doubt that securitizations will always trade at a discount. Of course, the securities trade in a different market than the underlying asset, so they have different risk-return characteristics. In some cases, the issuer could be creating value through that security, i.e. by providing liquidity and diversification benefits. Thus, the value of the security would be greater than the value of the underlying asset. Lack of information about the underlying real estate, however, may sometimes result in securities being undervalued.

QUESTION: Is there a valuation technique for appraising real estate portfolios besides summing the individual property appraisals?

FISHER: If one had the appropriate risk-return measures, real estate portfolios could be appraised with the same techniques used to value stocks and bonds. That value could be quite different than the sum of the values of the individual assets. The problem is that in many cases the institutional investor is required to value the portfolio on the basis of the market value of the individual assets, and hence does not have the flexibility of reporting a value that could be obtained by valuing the portfolio as a whole.

QUESTION: How do transfer structures that allow buyers to assume ownership without triggering real estate taxes or transfer taxes affect appraisals?

FISHER: I am not sure. But I have heard that in Chicago many buildings are set up as corporations. When a building is sold, the shares of stock are traded instead of the title to the real estate as a way to avoid the transfer tax. I do not know whether the value of the stock is the same as the value of the underlying real estate. This type of activity makes it very difficult to measure the value of the real estate.

QUESTION: Is it true that the values derived from each of the three appraisal approaches should be within 5 to 10 percent of one another?

FISHER: Often, three appraisers will not be within 5 to 10 percent of each other. Variation in the answer from different approaches will certainly depend on the type of property, market conditions, and the availability of information. There are no rules of thumb for how close the answers should be. When there are huge variations across the different approaches, however, it is usually because an appraiser is not accounting for something properly. For example, on a regional shopping center, the income approach may give a higher value than the cost approach, because the appraiser is not properly reducing the income to account for that portion attributable to the personal property and perhaps the business value. The income approach may produce a value that is much higher or much lower than the other approaches, depending on the owner's ability to lease the property properly. Most people would prefer to rely on the income approach, when used properly, as the best indication of value.

QUESTION: What are the prospects, over the next five years, for the development of good risk measures for real estate?

FISHER: I think we will have much better real estate risk measures in the future than we have now. Many efforts are underway to develop databases and indexes that will be able to generate these risk-return measures. That will, in turn, affect the valuation theory. The availability of better data will cause appraisers to modify the approaches that they use in valuing real estate. It may also force real estate appraisers to become more familiar with valuation techniques being used by security analysts for stocks and bonds. This will be a challenge for the appraisal profession.

Measurement of Risk in Real Estate

David L. McMillan

There are three reasons that real estate is appropriate for investment portfolios. First, it is generally accepted that real estate investments represent the single largest store of wealth in the world. Second, real estate is a good inflation hedge. And third, real estate provides good diversification. There is not much to say about the first reason; it is a fact. With regard to the second, real estate is a good inflation hedge because most rental agreements offer reasonably frequent opportunities to adjust rents upward, thereby passing increased taxes and operating expenses on to tenants. Investors should not expect the same level of invulnerability to inflation, however, over the next few years that they have experienced in the recent past, primarily because there is a large amount of unoccupied real estate in the United States. Until supply and demand become more closely aligned, rents cannot be expected to keep up with price increases in other sectors.

A good diversifier is one that improves the risk-reward rato of a portfolio. That is, when an asset is added to a portfolio, it improves return proportionately more than it increases risk exposure. The numerical proxies for reward and risk in this context are mean return and standard deviation of return, respectively. In this presentation, I will discuss the problems associated with these measures when they are used to evaluate real estate.

To determine the diversification value of real estate in portfolios, it is necessary to understand risk and return in the real estate market. Although there are many ways to calculate return, the basic idea is simple: return is the ending amount divided by the starting amount. The risk proxy is more difficult to identify. In most cases, standard deviation of return is used to measure risk. This measure may produce considerable variation in reported risk, sometimes because of the time period used to calculate subperiod returns. But, leaving this issue aside, it is useful to consider what standard deviation calculations are intended to measure: volatility. Using the standard deviation of portfolio returns in this manner assumes that the risk of investing in that portfolio is represented by the volatility of the portfolio price level, and that all of the information about the stocks in that portfolio is included in their closing prices.

This risk measure does not apply equally to equities and real estate. Probably the most widely used proxy for the equity market is the S&P 500. Its value is measured hundreds of times a day—or, at least, could be—and its ending values for the day, week, month, or quarter are used in countless calculations of risk and return. In the real estate market, risk measures are obtained using a similar methodology. Unfortunately, real estate prices are not always observed under the same conditions as stock prices. For example, in real estate, information about specific properties is not widely disseminated, whereas information is comparatively abundant on equity securities. Further, buildings, even landmark buildings, are not followed by a cadre of Wall Street analysts. Also, the trading frequency of property is extremely low. Hundreds of prices may be offered and accepted on a given stock on a given day; in property trading, a more typical pattern is that one price may be offered and one price accepted in thousands of days. In stock market transactions, only a small fraction of an issue's outstanding value will trade on any one day, setting the price that is used to measure return. In most real estate transactions, the entire property is sold at one time; marginal shares are not available. Finally, over the early period during which real estate endures its most significant risk—for example, zoning and other regulatory risks, financing risk, construction risk, leasing risk, and operating risk—pricing is often not available.

This pricing mechanism has important implications for the consideration of risk for an individual type of investment. The difference between stock and real estate pricing mechanisms will be reflected in the risk measures. Because it is important to be able to calculate the return on a real estate portfolio during periods when there have not been transactions, real estate portfolios are often priced artificially using appraisals—a method not commonly employed in the stock market. These property appraisals yield estimates of price, and, therefore, risk. Property appraisers take some of the same broad economic factors into account as stock market investors, but they are measuring the impact in different "spaces." Specifically, real estate risk is measured in "appraisal space" versus an "auction space."

It is possible to measure one phenomenon in two different ways and obtain two determinations, both of which have value. A homey example will illustrate this concept. As a child I spent a lot of time at the beach. Often, I swam out to an area where the water was about 10 feet over my head and treaded water. While there, I noticed changes in the tide. I sensed differences in the size of the swells and detected that the water level was changing or that the undercurrent was more or less than it had been earlier. I often turned so that I could see the shore, where my sisters were sunbathing or reading or whatever beachgoers who ignore the water do. Occasionally, I saw the people on the beach running around in incredible excitement, scurrying here and there, grabbing possessions, and fleeing because a large wave had pounded onto the shore with enough momentum to flood the entire encampment—sandwiches, blankets, and solitaire games. This, of course, was caused by a change in the tide.

Both my sisters and I were experiencing the same phenomenon, the coming of high tide. The change was perceptible to both of us, but in terms of their metric, which was the distance between themselves and wetness, the change was far more dramatic and action-packed than it was for me. My metrics were wave size and distance between the surface and the bottom. If I had told them of my observation that the water was one foot deeper than it had been an hour ago, it would have had little effect on their behavior, whereas if I had told them that the water was soon going to eat up 200 feet of dry sand, the news would have carried more meaning. Neither of our measurements was particularly flawed, but they were not usable for the same things.

It is dangerous to use a number, however good, in a process that yields unreasonable results. A perfect example of a number being misused is the standard deviation of a real estate return stream. Observers have noted that standard deviations derived from real property indexes are potentially misleading. Analysts, researchers, and academics have all commented on the fact that the most used institutional real estate index, the Frank Russell Company's FRC Property Index, indicates standard deviations that imply a risk level no one really believes—particularly when compared with the standard deviation of stocks and bonds. In fact, the real estate standard deviation is suspiciously close to the level of risk attributed to T-bills, and not at all close to that of stocks and bonds.

Many people have commented on the problems associated with the standard deviation of real estate

returns. Few people note, however, that there are similar problems with the correlation statistic. The formula for standard deviation is a simple function of variance, as shown in Figure 1, which in turn is derived from the mean corrected sum of squares. Figure 2 shows that the correlation is also dependent on the variance of real estate returns. If we have doubts about standard deviation (sigma), then we should also entertain doubts about correlation (rho).

To calculate the correlation between stocks and real estate, one must use the return numbers for both asset classes; the correlation is not meaningful, in my view, because the return numbers are not measured in the same way. Numbers measured in the same space—appraisal space, for example—are more

---

FIGURE 1. Standard Deviation Formula

$$\sigma_x = \text{var}(x)$$

Source: Frank Russell Company

FIGURE 2. Correlation Formula

$$\rho_{x,y} = \frac{\text{cov}(x,y)}{\text{var}(x)\text{var}(y)}$$

Source: Frank Russell Company

---

comparable and therefore more informative. Figure 3 shows four indexes of real estate returns in appraisal space: Texas, office, warehouse, and total real estate returns. The total index is the four-quarter moving return track of the FRC Property Index. In this case, the appraisal space numbers appear to make logical sense. The index for Texas real estate shows the poorest returns in recent years. One might also expect that the Texas rate of return would have more volatility than the total market because it is less well-diversified. We should be able to do asset allocation within region or within type, using these types of numbers, as long as we derive them in the same way. In Figure 4, the S&P 500 is superimposed on the real estate indexes; it shows that the S&P 500 is more volatile than even the Texas real estate market. That is a result that I am not sure would satisfy everyone.

Mean-variance optimization models using real estate numbers derived from the FRC Property Index or other appraisal-based rates of return generators

FIGURE 3. Real Estate: Four-Quarter Moving Returns

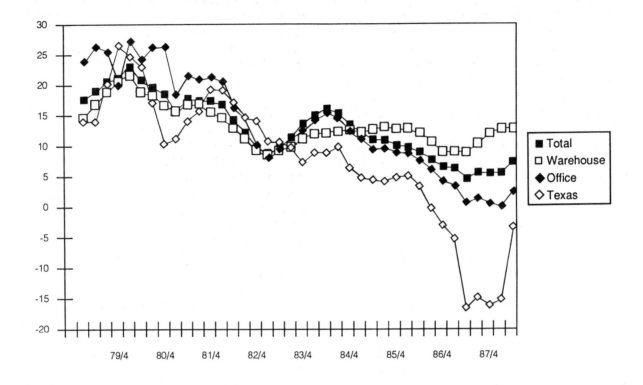

Source: Frank Russell Company

FIGURE 4. Real Estate versus S&P 500: Four-Quarter Moving Returns

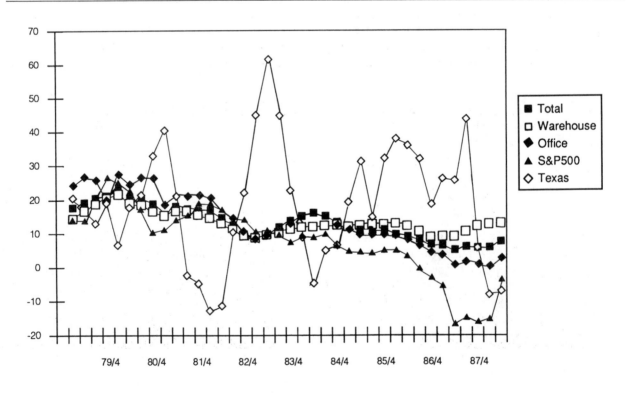

Source: Frank Russell Company

give challenging results. For example, using historical returns, standard deviation, and correlations of stocks, bonds, international equities, and real estate, a mean-variance optimization model would recommend that 80 or 90 percent of a portfolio be invested in real estate. Few advisors would be comfortable delivering this result to their clients, however, because it does not appear to make sense, indicating a lack of faith in either the method or the input. The most commonly used solution to this problem is to constrain real estate's allocation artificially to 10 or 15 percent of a portfolio, and then to optimize the rest of the portfolio freely.

EXPLORING REITs

The problems associated with real estate risk and return measurement outlined above have led me to research publicly traded real estate investment trusts (REITs) and related real estate securities as a proxy for the underlying real estate market. Although there are potential problems with using REITs and other stocks to represent real property, there are also, as we have seen, severe problems with current real estate valuation techniques.

Real estate stocks have several virtues. They trade in the same markets as other stocks and, hence, an index of these stocks should yield a risk number that is measured in the same space as other equities. Second, REITs have the attributes of real property. In particular, they produce cash with remarkable steadiness. Also, as Figure 5 demonstrates, they have a low beta, rarely even approaching one. (The three-year betas shown in the figure are the monthly returns to the National Association of Real Estate Investment Trusts Equity Index, versus the S&P 500 Total Return Index, in rolling 36-month periods.) The relation has varied quite a bit, but it has always stayed below one.

The figure shows a distinct downward trend since 1979. To determine where the trend originated, I plotted the components of beta: the correlation between stocks and REITs and the standard deviation of both stocks and REITs. Figure 6 shows the standard deviation of the S&P 500. The trend in standard deviation does not provide a clue as to why the betas have uniformly dropped for several years. Figure 7 shows the correlation between the S&P 500 and REITs. It has been reasonably steady, around 0.6, although the pattern over the past two to three years is suspiciously like the pattern of the betas. The downward trend is still unexplained. Figure 8 shows equity REIT standard deviations, illustrating a distinct 10-year decline in standard deviation. (The upward spikes following 1987 in all the graphs, of course, are caused by the events of October 1987.) Perhaps the falling REIT volatility reflects a growing perception by players in this market that they are dealing with real estate in a securitized form. This helps explain the 10-year decline in beta.

Real estate stock price behavior reflects the behavior of its underlying assets. This does not lead to the conclusion that all real property should be securitized, or that all pension funds should invest in securities rather than property, which would be impossible, given the size of the REIT securities market. It indicates that comparable risk estimates

FIGURE 5. Equity REIT Index versus S&P 500: Three-Year Beta

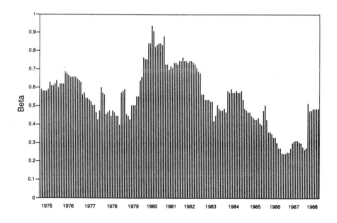

Source: Frank Russell Company

FIGURE 6. S&P 500 Standard Deviations

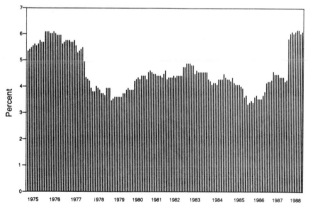

Source: Frank Russell Company

FIGURE 7. Equity REIT Index versus S&P 500: Three-year Correlations

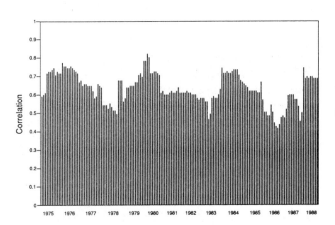

Source: Frank Russell Company

FIGURE 8. Equity REIT Standard Deviations

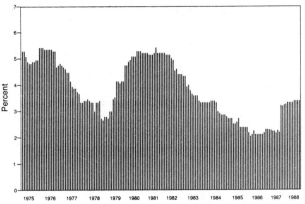

Source: Frank Russell Company

are more likely to be found in an actively traded auction market for real estate securities than in an index of appraised values. From an academic perspective, this conclusion is significant because these stocks may provide fertile ground for more research into the basic question of relative risk and, more importantly, into the asset allocations that pension plans should be making in real estate.

Nondirect Real Estate Investments

Michael T. Oliver, CFA

Evaluating real estate as an asset class within a portfolio of assets is difficult because real estate's characteristics are very different from those of other securities. Investing in publicly traded securities of real estate companies is free of many of the problems associated with direct investment in real estate. In this presentation, I will describe the advantages of investing in publicly traded real estate securities as an alternative to other equity real estate investments.

Publicly traded real estate securities resemble private real estate securities, such as commingled real estate funds, in many ways. For instance, the securities are owned by multiple investors, ownership is represented by a security interest, there are various reporting requirements, and their portfolios are actively managed. The significant difference between private and publicly traded securities is that the latter are priced in an auction market and must meet stringent Securities and Exchange Commission (SEC) reporting requirements.

The publicly traded real estate securities market is valued at approximately $60 billion and contains roughly 310 issues. These securities are represented by investment builders, equity real estate investment trusts (REITs), specialty real estate companies, limited partnerships (which could also be master limited partnerships), and real-estate-rich companies. The approximate number of issues and the market capitalization for each category of securities in the real estate securities industry is listed in Table 1. The list does not include debt-type companies—for example, collateralized mortgage obligations or mortgage REITs. The list does include investment builders who construct income-producing property that is not sold, but is valued by cash flow; equity real estate investment trusts that own property rather than mortgages; real estate companies, such as mortgage bankers; limited partnerships; and real-estate-rich companies, including landholding companies, such as Castle & Cooke, railroad companies such as Santa Fe Southern Pacific, and forest products companies. It has been jokingly argued that airlines are now real-estate-rich companies, because their landing slots and gates have become so valuable. Table 2 illustrates several examples of publicly traded real estate securities.

The ownership risks of real estate stocks are a combination of stock market and real estate risks. The basic risks in the ownership of common stock are interest-rate changes, general market conditions, and investor perceptions about an industry. This stock market risk can be mitigated partly by selling securities. Risks in real estate markets are local economic conditions, rent and operating expense levels, and competition. These risks can be mitigated through careful research that screens properties with unacceptably high risks relative to their anticipated returns.

THE CASE FOR PUBLICLY TRADED REAL ESTATE SECURITIES

There are several reasons why portfolio managers should consider the inclusion of publicly traded real estate securities in their investment portfolios. First, real estate securities are hybrid securities whose performance is similar to both equities and direct real estate ownership. Table 3 shows equity REIT returns versus both real estate returns and equity returns. The average return for the equity REIT has exceeded the average returns of both the S&P 500 and the Frank Russell Company Property Index over the past 10 years.

Second, publicly traded real estate securities should offer attractive opportunities to investors who are able to commit resources to research the market. Current Wall Street research on the real estate securities industry is incomplete and inaccurate. For example, fewer than 10 full-time Wall Street analysts follow equity REITs, which is approximately an $11 billion market. Coverage of these securities is very limited; analysts who follow real estate stocks typically cover only the so-called "nifty 15" companies, leaving the bulk of the industry uncovered from a research point of view.

Third, publicly traded real estate stocks are attractive securities for a number of reasons. The securities themselves offer both product and geographic diversification. The purchase of stock in several of these companies may provide instant diversification. These stocks also provide more liquidity than direct real estate investments—in fact, there is reasonable liquidity in even the smallest

TABLE 1. Publicly Traded Real Estate Securities Industry Summary

	Category	Market Capitalization ($ Billions)	Approximate Number of Issues
I.	Investment Builders	$4	40
II.	Equity Real Estate Investment Trusts	11	70
III.	Specialty Real Estate Companies	8	25
IV.	(Master) Limited Partnerships	4	30
V.	Real-Estate-Rich Companies	25	65
VI.	Other Real Estate Companies	8	80
	Totals	$60	310

Source: PRA Securities Advisors

companies. In addition, publicly traded real estate securities are generally listed on stock exchanges and must meet SEC reporting requirements. This is not true of private real estate securities.

Fourth, many of these securities sell at relatively high yields (currently 6 to 10 percent) and, therefore, do not require substantial price appreciation to provide attractive total returns. For some reason, the market does not pay a premium for management; many of these stocks sell at between 20 and 30 percent of their theoretical liquidation value. I believe that this will change as investors begin to understand the industry. In addition, a tremendous amount of information exists about local markets—about rents, about vacancy levels, and about other planned projects. The companies also provide information on the specific assets owned, so it is easier to analyze the income and expense numbers and determine cash flow.

One of the most important considerations for any security is whether management can add value. Many of the public real estate companies that have come to the market since 1985 have been nothing more than financing vehicles. The value added has been taken out, and the institutional investor is left with only a financing vehicle and very little return. Conversely, good management may increase value significantly. For example, we have had very good luck with companies doing a number of shopping center renovations. In many of these projects, the returns realized by the purchaser of the property far exceeded the original cost return, which had been around 10 percent.

REAL ESTATE INVESTMENT TRUSTS

REITs are only one of several categories of publicly traded real estate securities. Equity REITs own income-producing property and are valued on a net cash flow basis. Some equity REITs specialize in one type of property (i.e., shopping centers or apartments), while others specialize in specific geographic areas. Equity REITs share many of the general traits of publicly traded real estate securities; they provide income, appreciation—or, in some cases, depreciation—and diversification. These securities also have the advantage of liquidity, independent trustees representing the investors' interest, and regulation by the SEC and IRS.

In addition to equity REITs, there are several other types of REITs, including hybrid REITs, which are a combination of debt and equity; mortgage REITs; and specialty REITs, such as health care REITs. There are approximately 126 trusts which are actively traded, representing approximately $30 billion of assets and about $11 billion in market capitalization. Real estate must account for 75 percent of the income for a REIT, and trusts must hold the properties for the long term. In fact, if an equity REIT sells more than seven properties in any year, it may be disqualified for tax purposes. A REIT may be a self-managed company, or it may be managed by an advisory company. In general, REITs are run by professional management teams and provide competitive economic returns.

The 1986 Tax Reform Act eliminated many of the tax benefits of owning real estate. But the 1986 act

TABLE 2. Examples of Publicly Traded Real Estate Securities

Company Name	Stock Symbol	Exchange	Annual Dividend	6/30/88 Price	Yield	Shares Outstanding (Thousands)	Market Capitalization ($ Millions)
High-Yield Securities							
BRE Property	BRE	NYSE	$2.40	$30.50	7.9%	7,864	$239.9
Beverly Invest- ment Prop.	BIP	NYSE	2.36	14.25	16.6%	8,195	116.8
EQK Realty Investors I	EKR	NYSE	1.66	13.50	12.3%	7,589	102.5
Healthvest	HVT	ASE	2.52	20.75	12.1%	11,661	241.9
ICM Property Investors	ICM	NYSE	1.32	10.00	13.2%	5,695	56.9
Koger Property	KOG	NYSE	2.60	28.38	9.2%	12,429	352.7
Mtg & Realty Trust	MRT	NYSE	1.96	18.13	10.8%	10,597	192.1
Prop. Trust of America	PTRAS	OTC	0.80	9.38	8.5%	5,062	47.5
Turner Equity	TEQ	ASE	0.44	6.50	6.8%	5,607	32.9
Wells Fargo Mortgage	WFM	NYSE	1.50	17.38	8.6%	6,697	116.4
High Growth Securities							
Federal Realty	FRT	NYSE	1.20	20.88	5.8%	13,528	282.5
Rouse Co.	ROUS	OTC	0.52	22.50	2.3%	47,705	1,073.4
United Dominion Realty	UDRT	OTC	1.08	17.50	6.2%	7,968	139.4
Washington REIT	WRE	ASE	1.40	24.50	5.7%	9,182	224.9
Weingarten Realty	WRI	NYSE	1.68	27.13	6.2%	13,947	378.4
Real-Estate-Rich Companies							
Amfac	AMA	NYSE	0.00	46.50	0.0%	17,113	795.8
Castle & Cooke	CKE	NYSE	0.00	26.63	0.0%	47,378	1,261.7
Southern Pacific	SFX	NYSE	1.00	19.75	5.1%	157,106	3,102.8
Southmark Corp.	SM	NYSE	0.24	3.63	6.6%	46,020	167.1

Source: PRA Securities Advisors

was a major improvement for publicly traded real estate securities, particularly the REITs. The 1986 act broadened management functions; it permitted trusts to have subsidiaries, which is very important to some trusts; it permitted trusts to sell up to seven properties per year, compared to only three previously; and it expanded the ability of REITs to do joint ventures, making the REIT more flexible than it was prior to 1986.

REITs yield between 6 and 11 percent, on average. In many cases, the expected return of REITs exceeds that of the S&P 500. Figure 1 shows the yield for REITs versus the S&P 500 since 1978. REIT yields

have averaged between 7 and 9 percent, while the yield on the S&P 500 is between 3 and 6 percent. Interest rates during this period went from relatively low to very high and then back down again to relatively low, and yet the yields on the equity REITs, on an annualized basis, remained fairly constant.

Tables 4 and 5 show the correlation coefficients between real estate and the S&P 500. Table 4 shows the correlation of total returns over the period 1978-88. Table 5 shows the correlation of the income component of return from 1984 to 1988. The correlations suggest that equity REITs trade more similarly to stocks than to real estate, although some

TABLE 3. Historical Annual Performance Comparisons: Total Returns (1978-87)

Year	NAREIT Equity REIT Index	FRC Property Index	S&P 500 Index
1978	11.2%	16.0%	6.3%
1979	35.4	20.8	18.0
1980	17.2	18.1	31.3
1981	7.5	16.6	(5.0)
1982	17.0	9.4	20.3
1983	31.9	13.2	22.2
1984	16.3	13.1	5.9
1985	20.4	9.9	31.0
1986	18.5	6.3	18.5
1987	(3.5)	5.2	5.6
Mean	17.2%	12.9%	15.4%
Standard Deviation	10.6%	4.9%	11.3%

Sources: National Council of Real Estate Investment Fiduciaries; National Association of Real Estate Investment Trusts; Standard & Poor's Corporation; and PRA Securities Advisors

research suggests that that relation might be changing. Although we have not made enough observations to corroborate this finding fully, we feel that over an 8- to 15-year period, the value of the publicly traded real estate securities will track the value of the underlying real estate. The Rouse Company, for example, has been publishing fair

market value for a number of years, and the stock price tends to track that value.

VALUING REAL ESTATE SECURITIES

There are several steps in valuing real estate securities. First, the type of business to be invested in must be determined. This requires asking a lot of questions. For example, should shopping centers, office buildings, or apartments be owned? Should the investment be in the land development business or the homebuilding business?

Second, the companies that best fit the chosen business category must be indentified. This process narrows the universe of possible investments to a manageable size.

Third, the companies must be visited to learn their strategy, their accounting functions, and their budgeting procedures. At the same time, written material must be studied—annual reports, filings with the SEC, and Wall Street research. Good management and dynamic growth are important in the real estate portfolio, and the current yield and growth prospects should be examined.

The final step is to calculate a competitive

FIGURE 1. Equity REIT Yields versus S&P Yield

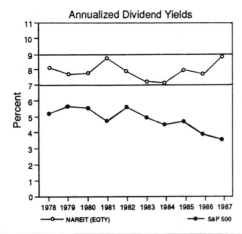

Sources: National Association of Real Estate Investment Trusts; Standard & Poor's Corporation; and PRA Securities Advisors

TABLE 4.	Correlation Coefficients—Quarterly Total Returns (1978 - 1Q 1988)		
	NAREIT	S&P 500	FRC
NAREIT	1.000	0.744	(0.012)
S&P 500		1.000	(0.127)
FRC			1.000

NOTE: This correlation is based on quarterly time-weighted rates of return which measure the change in value during the quarter, expressed as a percentage of beginning period market value for each index.

Sources: National Council of Real Estate Investment Fiduciaries; National Association of Real Estate Investment Trusts; Standard & Poor's Corporation; and PRA Securities Advisors

risk-adjusted return. If the expected rate of return for the most stable companies in the business (e.g., investment builders) is 15 percent, then the return for more risky companies (developers) would have to be higher, for example at the 19 to 20 percent level, because the risk is higher.

CONCLUSION

To summarize, publicly traded real estate securities

TABLE 5.	Correlation Coefficients—Quarterly Income Component (1984 - 1Q 1988)		
	NAREIT	S&P 500	FRC
NAREIT	1.000	0.898	0.694
S&P 500		1.000	0.772
FRC			1.000

NOTE: This correlation is derived from the quarterly dividend yield during the quarter, based on a standardized price index for each series.

Sources: National Council of Real Estate Investment Fiduciaries; National Association of Real Estate Investment Trusts; PRA Securities Advisors

provide investors the opportunity to choose their own destiny. They allow investors to trade their own securities and balance their portfolios. These securities provide liquidity in excess of the liquidity provided by direct ownership of real estate, as well as competitive economic returns. The publicly traded real estate securities market is not large enough to accommodate all of the available pension fund money. Therefore, we view this market as an adjunct to, or a single component in, a comprehensive real estate investment program.

Question and Answer Session

QUESTION: Would you please describe the FRC Property Index?

MCMILLAN: The FRC Property Index is an index of about 1,000 institutionally held, tax-exempt, wholly owned, income-producing properties in the United States. They are existing properties entailing no development, and no debt. The data are collected every quarter from the members of NCREIF and include each property's income for the quarter, capital improvements made during the period, market value, and whether any partial sales were made during that time. The Frank Russell Company calculates a rate of return and produces an index from those data. This index is probably the only direct real estate proxy that can be considered impartial.

QUESTION: Have you attempted to measure the FRC Index against any other stock market index, such as the Wilshire 5000? If so, could you comment on the results?

MCMILLAN: We have made such comparisons. It does not matter what index you use; you can put 50 asset classes in an asset allocation algorithm, but it will still select a huge proportion of real estate because the relative risk, as measured by this index, is so low. The risk-reward trade-off is so large that real estate will be grabbed by almost any optimization model.

QUESTION: If one uses REIT statistics as a proxy to the characteristics of the real estate market, what percentage of a portfolio will be allocated to real estate?

MCMILLAN: That is an excellent question. Mike Oliver showed that REITs had higher returns and lower risk than the S&P 500, which indicates that no asset allocation model is going to select the S&P 500 if those numbers are used as inputs for the risk-return trade-off.[1] There is still a huge gap between what we have found and what we can actually use. Investing directly in the property market is not a tenable way to do asset allocation, in the mean variance sense. But, by the same token, strict use of REIT numbers will not provide the right asset allocation for buying property either.

[1]See Mr. Oliver's presentation, pp. 29 - 33.

QUESTION: Why would one want to invest in an equity REIT that has a correlation to the S&P 500 of 0.6 or 0.7, when a direct investment in real estate has virtually a zero correlation with equities?

MCMILLAN: I do not believe that the correlation between equities and real estate is zero. If all direct property in the country changed hands once a day, the real estate risk and return numbers would be very different—not so smooth. Of course, we will never know how property would act under these conditions. Measuring these values in two completely different markets is a thorny issue for investors who want to know the optimal amount of real estate to buy.

QUESTION: Does an investor in REITs give up the long-term illiquidity premium of direct real estate investments?

OLIVER: Whether there is a premium for owning real estate directly is not an issue. A security bought at a 9 percent yield that has a 6 percent expected growth rate in cash flow over the next three to five years should yield a 15 percent rate of return. That is how I measure it.

QUESTION: REITs with lower market capitalizations seem to sell at significant discounts to those with higher capitalizations. Is this justified, or is it an opportunity for superior returns?

OLIVER: The difference illustrates my point that this industry is underresearched. Clearly, large capitalization stocks have a fairly large following, and the major analysts on Wall Street do follow them and know them fairly well. But they only know what management says; very few of those investors go out and look at the properties. The smaller capitalization stocks provide some tremendous opportunity over a period of time, and that is important, because real estate securities are evaluated over a 10- to 15-year period, not on a quarter-by-quarter basis. An investor who is willing to accept a 10- to 15-year time horizon should consider a $20 million REIT, because at some point the yield will get high enough to force the stock price up to the point where new equity or convertible debt can be sold, and that $20 million REIT will become a $100 million REIT. Size should not be a criteria; however, because the discounts are greater—and the yields are higher—such an investment has appreciation potential over a period of time.

QUESTION: How do you explain the decision by several REIT managers to liquidate their portfolios in lieu of continuing as an operating company?

OLIVER: The answer lies with the managements of those trusts and whether the trusts were truly adding value or were just financing vehicles. I think that some of the groups liquidating now—for example, Property Capital Trust, Money Investors, and Wells Fargo—were pure financing vehicles. There was no real value added to the product. As a consequence, investors were not willing to pay the same price for their securities as they were for the more developmental or entrepreneurial type companies, so yields became so high that the managers could not put the money to work. The industry has a history of forming and liquidating trusts. New equity real estate investment trusts and REITs are still being formed, and other REITs are being de-formed.

QUESTION: How do you manage the unsystematic risk in a portfolio of REITs, that is, the risk that varies over property type and geographic region?

OLIVER: I wish that there were something we *could* manage, but we do not. We consider the track record of the management, what is happening in that particular market, and whether that is a market that we want to be in and a team that we want to be with. Right now, our portfolio includes about 300 properties of broadly diversified product type and broadly diversified geographic type, and it is virtually impossible to measure any kind of risk on that basis.

QUESTION: That broad a mix of properties may provide diversification in a real estate sense, but does it provide diversification in a stock market sense?

OLIVER: We are not concerned about diversification in the stock market sense. Research indicates that using equity REITs in a stock portfolio lowers risk and improves the expected rate of return.

Management of the Asset Allocation Decision

Denis S. Karnosky

Investors are broadening their perspectives on the range of asset classes to be included in portfolios. In this context, optimal allocation within a portfolio becomes an important decision. I will focus on the allocation decision at the policy level—that is, which assets to invest in and in what proportion. It is also important to be aware of issues relating to day-to-day portfolio management and operation. Within the context of a portfolio, I will discuss why real estate should be considered in addition to other assets.

Real estate is one asset class within the broad market of investable capital. The U.S. investment capital market is estimated to be slightly over $9 trillion, and is approximately 40 percent dollar-denominated bonds, approximately 29 percent equity, more than 16 percent equity real estate, approximately 14 percent cash equivalents, and less than 1 percent venture capital, as shown in Figure 1. The real estate class is limited to those sectors that are most suited to pension fund investments, including nonfarm, noncorporate, and equity real estate. If this horizon is broadened to include the global investable capital market, adding nondollar bonds and non-U.S. equities, the domestic real estate share of the total drops to about 7.6 percent on a market-weighted basis. Figure 2 illustrates the composition of the total investable capital market in 1987.

Ideally, the most efficient, broadly diversified portfolio consists of "the market." The difficulty is that no two investors are alike in terms of time horizons, liability structures, tax situations, legal constraints, trade-offs between risks and rewards, or even in their perceptions of the economy. This problem has led us to derive the Multiple Markets Index (MMI)—a measure of what the market is or what kind of weights would be expected for a "typical" U.S. investor. The MMI portfolio allocation is shown in Figure 3. The idea behind the MMI is to take the assets that comprise the investable capital market and combine them in a risk-return structure that approximates the preferences of a typical U.S. pension fund. In terms of traditional domestic securities, that would be a portfolio holding about 60 percent in domestic equities and 40 percent in domestic bonds, with perhaps a small amount of cash. According to our estimates, an MMI portfolio with a 15 percent real estate holding generates a risk structure approximating that of a 60/40 stock-bond portfolio, but offers a higher expected normal return—between 50 and 100 basis points higher, on average.

Table 1 shows the actual performance of each of the assets that comprise the investable capital market from 1969 to the end of 1987. Among all of the asset classes in our broadest portfolio—domestic equities, foreign equities, venture capital, dollar bonds, international dollar bonds, nondollar bonds, real estate, and cash—the reported historical risk-return characteristics of real estate are the most attractive. The measured return on real estate is slightly under 11 percent and the volatility is 2.5 percent.

Based on the historical data in Table 1, real estate is a very attractive asset. There are good reasons to doubt whether these historical data accurately represent the true risk-return dynamics of the equity real estate market, however. Using the historical risk measure to proxy the risk in the future would be very foolish. The obvious advantage of historical returns is that they are known and may be measured. But if the period over which the returns in Table 1 were measured is examined more closely, unique historical phenomena become apparent: Richard Nixon was President at the beginning of this period; he was followed by Gerald Ford, Jimmy Carter, and Ronald Reagan. The Shah of Iran died, OPEC shot its bolt, the Vietnam War ended, the Federal Reserve ceased to be a basic inflationary force in the economy and, in fact, turned the other way. Using history as a guide to the future assumes that the phenomena that generated the historical observations will be repeated in the immediate future. No one believes that will happen, of course, which suggests that historical numbers should not be used blindly as indications of probable future conditions. Historical data apply only to the specific period in which they occurred, and there is no reason to believe that any

FIGURE 1. **FIGURE 1. U.S. Investable Capital Market
(12/31/87)**

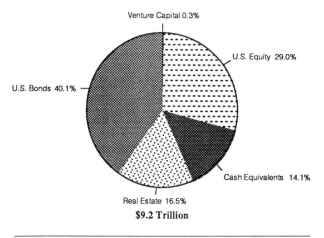

$9.2 Trillion

Source: First Chicago Investment Advisors

**FIGURE 2. Total Investable Capital Market
(12/31/87)**

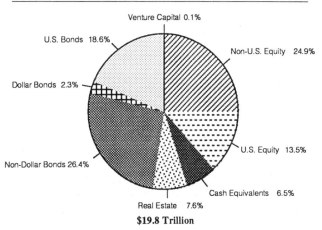

$19.8 Trillion

Source: First Chicago Investment Advisors

of the observed time-series properties of these data will persist in the immediate future.

Does that mean that history is irrelevant? Of course not. It does mean, however, that historical data must be screened and analyzed for information content. What do the data tell us? Do we know what impact a change in the inflation rate will have on asset returns, volatility, or correlations? Do we understand what it means to start a period with fixed exchange rates and move into one with floating rates? Can we identify the impacts of changes in tax policy and regulatory environment on the data? If the effects of such external phenomena can be identified, then the historical observations begin to provide insight into the internal dynamics of the market.

The historical data from Table 1 are plotted in Figure 4. The MMI plots near the center of the graph,

FIGURE 3. Multiple Markets Index

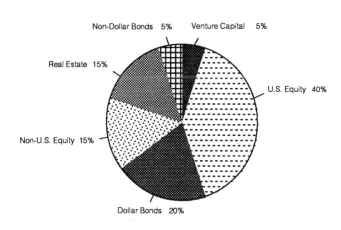

Source: First Chicago Investment Advisors

with an actual return of about 12 percent and a volatility of about 13 percent over the period from 1970 to 1987. From these historical data, it appears that real estate has made cash a redundant asset. In fact, real estate effectively dominates the entire domestic fixed-income market. Why would one ever want to hold dollar bonds or domestic bonds, considering the apparently superior risk-return trade-off that is offered by real estate?

Table 2 shows the historical correlation matrix for the asset classes that comprise the investable capital market. The table shows that real estate is not positively correlated with the other assets. In fact, the highest correlations are 0.15 with venture capital and 0.08 with U.S. equity; real estate is negatively correlated with the other asset classes. Therefore, according to historical data, real estate has a high return, a low volatility, and a negative covariance against most assets. Is it any surprise that portfolio optimizers who use historical data will love real estate? Any optimization model that uses historical data as input will recommend an overinvestment in real estate. To override this solution, most people establish an artificial limit for real estate in the portfolio of perhaps 10 to 15 percent. The optimizer then selects the remainder of the portfolio from the less optimal asset classes. The result is thus guaranteed to be suboptimal.

Table 3 shows our estimates of the *equilibrium* returns and risks for the various asset classes. In determining the optimal multiasset portfolio, we use a long-term real estate return of 10.2 percent and a risk factor of 14 percent. The 14 percent volatility number is approximately six times larger than the historical number. The expected return estimate consists of three parts: (1) a real rate of return, which should be common to all asset classes, of 1.4 percent;

(2) an inflation premium, which should also be common to all asset classes, of 5 percent; and (3) a risk premium of 3.8 percent. These estimates are the result of several processes, including analysis of historical data, the judgment of investment professionals, and quantitative methods.

The equilibrium correlation forecasts shown in Table 4 show that real estate is estimated to have a relatively low correlation with equities and fixed-income securities, but significantly higher than the data for the period since the 1960s would indicate. In fact, estimated correlations against equities are in the 30 to 35 percent range: against fixed-income securities, estimated correlations are in the 15 to 20 percent range. The only correlation that follows the historical trend is the small negative correlation with cash.

Figure 5 shows two attainable efficient frontiers. The solid line is the standard domestic stock-bond-cash efficient frontier; the dotted line is the efficient frontier for the broader set of assets as represented by the MMI portfolio. The return increment added by real estate is probably worth about 20 to 25 basis points at low levels of risk, declining 15 to 20 basis points at higher levels of risk. A portfolio with 60 percent domestic stocks and 40 percent bonds has an implied risk level of about 12 percent, the same as MMI. At that level of portfolio risk, the forecast returns, risks, and correlations imply an optimal real estate weight (unconstrained) of 15 percent.

Figure 6 shows the cumulative performance of the MMI versus real estate since 1970. Until very recently, real estate had outperformed the broader market. Overall, it is a very good performing market until the mid-1980s, when real estate has, on average, been a severe underperformer.

ASSET MANAGEMENT

Whether portfolio managers add value through active stock selection or timing decisions is an important question. Figure 7 shows a matrix

TABLE 1. INVESTABLE CAPITAL MARKET PERFORMANCE CHARACTERISTICS 12/31/69 - 12/31/87

	Mean Annual Returns		Standard Deviation (*)
	Arithmetic	Geometric	
Equities:			
U.S. Equity	12.3%	10.2%	19.9%
Total Non-U.S. Equity	17.0	14.8	19.4
Venture Capital	19.9	12.6	35.9
Fixed-Income Securities:			
Domestic Bonds	9.8	9.4	8.2
International Dollar Bonds	10.2	10.0	6.7
Non-Dollar Bonds	13.5	12.7	12.3
Real Estate (U.S.)	10.7	10.7	2.4
Cash Equivalents (U.S.)	7.6	7.6	1.3
Investable Capital Market Portfolio	11.4	10.9	9.1
MMI	12.6	11.8	12.6
60% Stock/40% Bond Index	11.3	10.3	13.5
Inflation (PCE)	6.1	6.1	1.4

*Standard deviation of quarterly logarithmic returns, annualized
Source: First Chicago Investment Advisors

FIGURE 4. MMI and Passive Indexes (1970-1987)

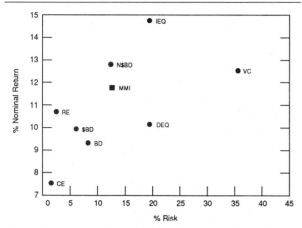

Annualized Logarithmic Standard Deviation based on quarterly data.

Source: First Chicago Investment Advisors

framework used to analyze managerial activity for a large sample of pension plans over the period from 1973 to 1983. The lower righthand corner of the figure, labeled Quadrant I, shows the average return to passively managed portfolios, in which the assets are held at fixed weights over the period. This portfolio would have generated a return of 10.11 percent. By manipulating the specific investments in stocks and bonds, and by manipulating the mix between them, the average portfolio manager succeeded in losing 110 basis points. By allowing portfolio managers to control the timing of asset allocation, the average return drops from 10.1 percent (Quadrant I) to 9.4 percent (Quadrant II). Active management in the selection of specific stocks

and bonds decreased the average return from 10.1 to 9.75 percent. The combination of both timing and selection drops the average return down to 9 percent (Quadrant IV).

The point is not that stock selection and asset allocation are necessarily bad, but that long-term results will be dominated by the initial asset allocation policy decision. The weight assigned to assets in the initial portfolio accounts for most of the performance. We are in the process of updating this study through 1987. The preliminary results are about the same: There is a small positive contribution from security selection, but market timing appears to detract from performance.

Thus, the decision to include real estate should be made first at the policy level; over long periods of time, that decision will probably dominate the contribution of real estate to the total performance of the portfolio. The investment may then be managed to add value, but only at a level that is determined primarily by the initial policy decision.

There are several problems with real estate investments in a multiportfolio context: transaction costs are very high relative to other asset classes, the data are not as good, the cost of information is high, and the cost of correcting mistakes is very high. Real estate transactions tend to be microanalyzed. Is this a good property? Is this a good deal? The top-down, macroconsistency, portfolio aspect of the decision tends to be overlooked. The critical consideration is whether an investment is attractive *relative to the other assets in the portfolio,* and even relative to another piece of property. Real estate investments are not good or bad, in an absolute sense, they are better or worse than some alternatives. From a portfolio

TABLE 2. Investable Capital Market Correlation Matrix*

	1	*2*	*3*	*4*	*5*	*6*	*7*	*8*	*9*	*10*
1. U.S. Equity	1.00									
2. Non-U.S. Equity	.69	1.00								
3. Venture Capital	.63	.51	1.00							
4. Domestic Bonds	.41	.33	.12	1.00						
5. International $ Bonds	.47	.42	.23	.96	1.00					
6. Nondollar Bonds	.24	.62	.25	.54	.55	1.00				
7. Real Estate	.08	-.05	.15	-.12	-.11	-.15	1.00			
8. Cash Equivalents	-.10	-.27	.07	-.03	-.05	-.33	.58	1.00		
9. Investable Capital Market Portfolio	.82	.86	.58	.65	.70	.70	.00	-.20	1.00	
10. Multiple Markets Index	.97	.79	.71	.51	.58	.43	.06	-.14	.92	1.00

* Based on Quarterly Logarithmic Returns (12/31/69-12/31/87)
Source: First Chicago Investment Advisors

TABLE 3.	Long-Term Asset Class Equilibrium Returns		

Asset Class	Equilibrium Return	Risk
U.S. Equity	12.0%	17.5%
Non-U.S. Equity	11.8	19.5
Venture Capital	18.5	45.0
Dollar Bonds	8.1	7.5
Non-Dollar Bonds	8.2	9.0
Real Estate	10.2	14.0
Cash Equivalents	6.4	1.5
Multiple Markets Index	11.1%	11.9%

Source: First Chicago Investment Advisors

FIGURE 5. **Attainable Efficient Frontiers**

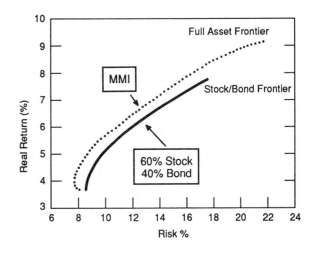

Source: First Chicago Investment Advisors

manager's perspective, the key to real estate investing is to make a decision on a particular piece of property within a real estate portfolio context, and then within a portfolio context relative to all other assets that are held. Evaluating real estate relative to the rest of a portfolio requires discipline and an internal investment structure that considers real estate within the context of all of the other asset class decisions. Making real estate decisions first and then trying to fit them into a portfolio will not work in a multiasset portfolio; the resulting portfolio will be suboptimal. Simply investing in another asset class, especially one that is project-specific like real estate, does not provide automatic diversification. There is a very good chance that the investment will be a redundant asset—an asset already represented in the

portfolio. Real estate in the oil patch, for example, is much like an energy stock; and if the equity managers are dumping all of those stocks because they are aware of that and real estate investors are taking them on, the portfolios have not been improved.

CONCLUSION

Establishing the normal real estate portion of the portfolio is the dominant decision, and different managers will do better or worse in managing around that over time. The real estate decision must be made in a portfolio context, and must be integrated into the process. Failing to evaluate real

TABLE 4. Long-Term Asset Class Equilibrium Returns: Correlation Forecasts*							
	1	2	3	4	5	6	7
1. U.S. Equity	1.00						
2. Non-U.S. Equity	.60	1.00					
3. Venture Capital	.35	.15	1.00				
4. Dollar Bonds	.45	.25	.15	1.00			
5. Non-Dollar Bonds	.25	.60	.10	.30	1.00		
6. Real Estate	.35	.30	.25	.20	.15	1.00	
7. Cash Equivalents	-.10	-.15	-.10	-.05	-.10	.20	1.00

* Annual returns
Source: First Chicago Investment Advisors

FIGURE 6. Multiple Markets Index

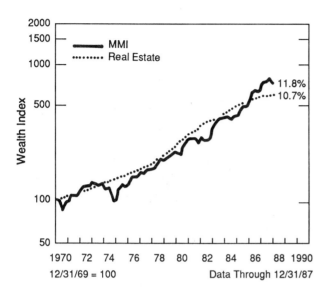

Source: First Chicago Investment Advisors

FIGURE 7. Mean Annualized Returns by Activity, 91 Large Plans (1974-1983)

Selection

	Actual	Passive
Actual	(IV) 9.01%	(II) 9.44%
Passive	(III) 9.75%	(I) 10.11%

Timing

Active Returns Due to:

Timing	-0.66%
Security Selection	-0.36
Other	-0.07
Total Active Return	-1.10%

Source: Gary P. Brinson, L. Randolph Hood, and Gilbert L. Beebower, "Determinants of Portfolio Performance," *Financial Analysts Journal*, (July/August 1986).

estate investments through the eyes of the equity manager or the fixed-income manager may easily result in suboptimal management of what might otherwise be a very efficient, productive asset class.

Management of the Asset Allocation Decision

Susan Hudson-Wilson, CFA

The concept of managing real estate investments as a portfolio is new in the real estate investment industry. The concept is overdue, and it is being developed now because real estate is no longer considered a nontraditional investment area. As interest in the asset class rises, so does the demand for sophisticated and objective analysis.

The primary goal in managing real estate investments is to achieve superior returns. Figure 1 illustrates the two approaches to achieving that goal: (1) making the best individual investments, and (2) intelligent, objective portfolio design. Most traditional real estate investing has focused on the individual investment aspect. Clearly, it is important: If you cannot pick good investments, you do not belong in the business. Portfolio design, however, is critical to the success of a real estate investment program. Good investments may be enhanced or offset by the design of the portfolio.

Real estate research is the foundation of both individual investments and portfolio design. Finding good individual investments is complicated. Careful project analysis, fed by an in-depth understanding of local markets, is only one of many dimensions of that process. I believe that it is a critical dimension, however. On the other side, portfolio design requires objective information on market returns and volatility at a very detailed level, and that information must be comparable over structure type, geographic area, and time.

REAL ESTATE RESEARCH

Real estate research is a broad topic. I would like to describe the work being done at John Hancock Properties to illustrate the importance of research in this industry. Our research efforts involve economic analysis, focusing on analysis at the urban and county level, rather than the regional level. It is not sufficient to analyze markets only at the regional level because real estate markets are principally local in nature. Research in real estate has both qualitative and quantitative aspects. We probably use a more quantitative approach than most firms do.

It is important to incorporate objectivity into the research, and to set some standards which may be applied across different locations and time periods. There are four principles which guide our research efforts. First, we emphasize applied research, not theoretical; although we like to work with the academic community as much as possible, we need ideas that may be used immediately. We do not have time to pursue interesting paths that may not generate superior returns. Second, we are developing knowledge and insight to exploit inefficiencies (we believe markets are inefficient). Third, we seek to achieve meaningful diversification and to develop guidelines which may be implemented. We consider both the demand and supply sides of the market. The demand side is only 50 percent of the problem; the other 50 percent may blindside you at any moment. Fourth, we try to be very accurate in our forecasting.

The success of research efforts is dependent on the quality of the underlying data. Real estate data comes in two forms: One is idiosyncratic data, the other systematic data. Idiosyncratic data—for example, the vacancy rates produced by local brokerage houses—is interesting, but we do not rely on it. We collect the data, examine it, and use it to the extent that it is useful, but the data are not comparable across space; each source has its own collection and calculation techniques. An analyst must ask all data sources to explain their methods. Systematic data, in contrast, are available over time, over geographic area, and over property types. Ideally, the data should be highly disaggregated by geography and by property type; they should bear a close relation to real estate returns; and they should be reliable enough to use in forecasting conditions within any particular real estate market.

The real estate industry does not have a good statistic for evaluating the markets. To fill the void, we created our own proxy for real estate returns: the John Hancock Real Estate Market Indicator (JHREMI). This indicator is really a marginal vacancy rate; the structure of the statistic relates changes in supply to changes in demand. This statistic is quite volatile, which is good because it is

FIGURE 1. The Means to Superior Returns

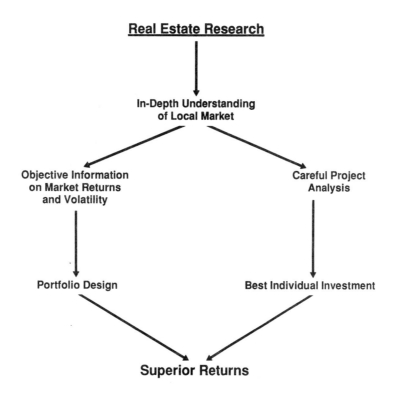

Real Estate Research

In-Depth Understanding
of Local Market

Objective Information
on Market Returns
and Volatility

Careful Project
Analysis

Portfolio Design

Best Individual Investment

Superior Returns

Source: John Hancock Properties, Inc. Real Estate Research

sensitive to activity in the market. The JHREMI statistic incorporates the economic structure of a market, changes in the economic structure, the growth rate of an economy, the intensity of space use, and a submarket analysis. It is important to understand the economic structure and the dynamics of markets as well as changes in the economic structure and the persistence of these changes. The submarket analysis addresses individual property types within a given metropolitan area or county.

One cannot rely on historical data to analyze a market. The growth rate of an economy and the intensity of space use vary over time and economic conditions, both nationally and locally. They also vary by property type and as the style of a market changes. Jacksonville, Florida is probably the best example of a city that has recently undergone an interesting transition from a small, backwater economy to a far more important regional economy. Over that transition, the intensity of space use has changed dramatically as well. Relying on history to analyze space use would be wrong, because the structure of the market is changing.

The JHREMI statistic incorporates a submarket analysis covering 60 cities and five structure types within those cities. The five structure types are apartments, office, retail, warehouse, and research and development. Typically, we examine several breakdowns of the data—for example, apartment complexes with more than 200 units or office buildings between three and six stories. This analysis may be taken down to the county level, which is important because most metropolitan areas include more than one county. Thus, the ability to analyze data on a county level allows us to address some of the submarket issues. This ability to sort the data allows us to focus specifically on a project and thereby understand our competition.

The characteristics of JHREMI are appealing. First, it is consistent over time, space, and property type. Second, it is forecastable in its separate parts: the demand and supply sides may be forecast separately and then combined, allowing for sensitivity analysis. For example, different economic environments and different types of supply constraints may be explored and then the net effect of these two events can be examined. Third, the statistic is positively correlated with vacancy rates. Fourth, the statistic is negatively correlated with real estate returns. Finally, the statistic is a leading indicator of both vacancy rates and real estate returns.

This statistic is used to compare markets objectively, to anticipate turning points, and to construct optimal portfolios. We have recently calibrated the JHREMI to returns, and now can express it in a vacancy rate context or in a rate of return context; each is the mirror image of the other.

THE DEVELOPMENT OF THE DATA

The way to achieve superior portfolio performance is to combine property types and locations, providing the greatest return for the least risk. The following example will illustrate the way that local real estate returns are estimated and forecast.

The project under consideration is an apartment building in Riverside-San Bernardino, California. The analysis begins with an examination of the population trends in the consolidated metropolitan area of Los Angeles. (Riverside is very much integrated with that larger area.) Figure 2 shows that population growth has been quite strong lately. We forecast that trend will continue near current peak levels into the future.

The second step is to analyze the Riverside-San Bernardino market within that metropolitan area.

As Figure 3 illustrates, the population growth as a percentage of the Los Angeles area is pretty dramatic. Next, we analyze the economics of the market. Because this is an apartment property, we question the relative cost of owning versus renting and the population's propensity to rent versus own. The demographics of the market are also considered. The demand side is broken down into individual age cohorts, which are then weighted, depending on their propensity to rent. For example, the cohort between the ages of 18 and 34 has a far higher propensity to rent than the cohort between the ages of 45 and 55, so that cohort is weighted more heavily. The older cohort—65 years old and older—is also weighted more heavily, because people in that age group are more likely to rent. In Riverside-San Bernardino, one would expect a higher-than-usual share of the renter cohort, because the population is growing so rapidly. In this case, that is true. This community is light in the sector that owns; there is a higher proportion of 18- to 34-year-old people and a higher than usual proportion of people over 65.

The demand side is only 50 percent of the story, however. To analyze the supply side, we review contract awards for apartments in the metropolitan area and by county. In this case, we examined

---

FIGURE 2. Population: Los Angeles SCA—Annual Increase

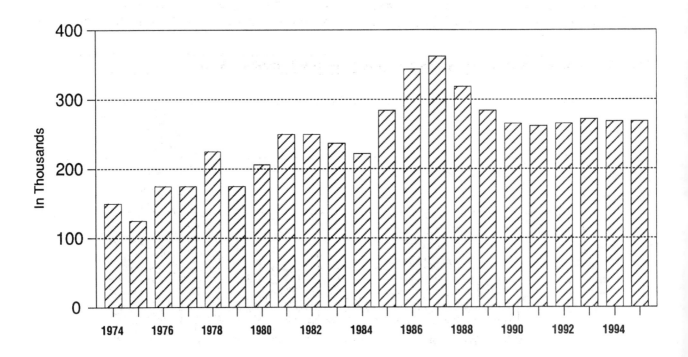

Source: Data Resources and John Hancock Properties, Inc. Real Estate Research

FIGURE 3. Population: Riverside-San Bernardino as a share of the Los Angeles SCA

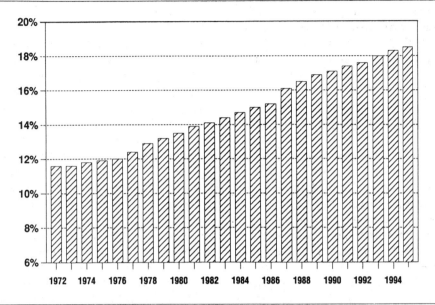

Source: Data Resources and John Hancock Properties Inc. Real Estate Research

Riverside and San Bernardino counties separately. Figure 4 indicates that this market has changed. Riverside-San Bernardino was a backwater community for awhile, but it has become a very active place since 1984. It appears that population growth is driving activity. Contract awards fell off quite markedly, however, beginning in 1987.

The demand and supply analyses are interesting, but one needs to know how they are working together. In Figure 5, the two sides of the market are combined with an algorithm, creating the JHREMI. The statistic shows that the Riverside-San Bernardino market is very volatile: It was very soft in 1978, very tight in 1980, and has deteriorated steadily ever since. Demand has been terrific, but supply has been too strong relative to demand. The good news is that a turning point is anticipated in 1990. If the JHREMI turns in 1990, vacancy rates and returns should turn in 1991. With this information, we may set some policy with respect to our behavior

FIGURE 4. Contract Awards for Apartments: Riverside-San Bernardino MSA

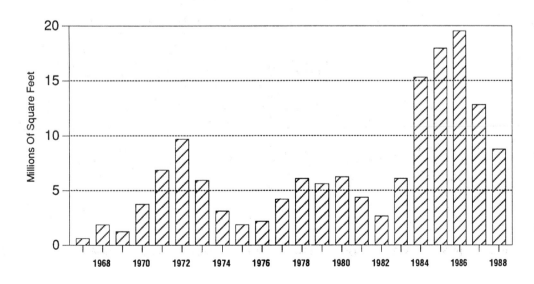

Source: F.W. Dodge

FIGURE 5. Apartment Market Outlook: Riverside-San Bernardino MSA

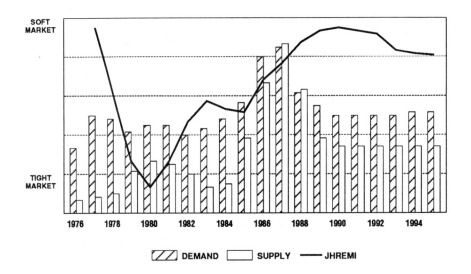

Source: John Hancock Properties Inc. Real Estate Research

in this market.

Different market volatilities may be compared using the JHREMI. Not all markets have the same degree of volatility. Figure 6 shows the Riverside-San Bernardino apartment market and the Seattle apartment market. San Bernardino has been volatile, but slightly less so than Seattle. Anyone familiar with Boeing's effect on Seattle is probably not surprised to see that. The Seattle market peaked in terms of its JHREMI value in 1985, which means the

vacancy rates peaked and returns troughed in 1986, and have improved since that time. The Riverside-San Bernardino market has a different cycle.

It is interesting to see how the JHREMI statistic correlates with other industry statistics. Figure 7 shows the JHREMI statistic versus the Coldwell Banker vacancy rates. The JHREMI statistic is a leading indicator of vacancy rates. For example, in 1979 the JHREMI began to rise before the Coldwell

FIGURE 6. Apartment JHREMI

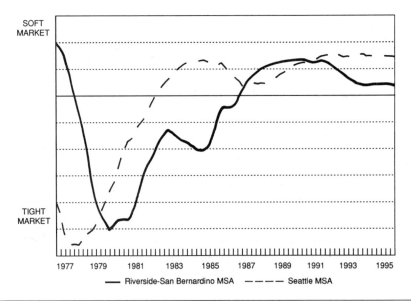

Source: John Hancock Properties Inc. Real Estate Research

FIGURE 7. JHREMI Versus Coldwell Banker Vacancy Rates: U.S. Office Market

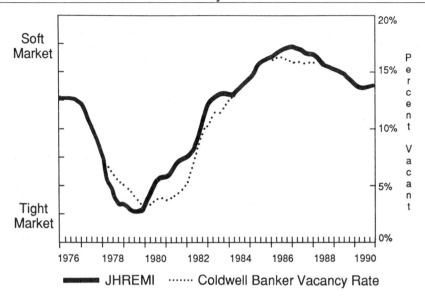

Source: John Hancock Properties Inc. Real Estate Research

Banker vacancy rates. The JHREMI started to fall in 1987; vacancy rates should be falling now, and we expect them to fall gently for the next couple of years. Figure 8 shows a plot of the JHREMI for office markets versus the Frank Russell Company quarterly total real returns for offices. These two indexes are negatively correlated, as evidenced by the pattern of the plots.

THE INVESTMENT DECISION-MAKING PROCESS

I would now like to describe a procedure for making well-informed individual investment decisions. The basis for our decisions is an extensive database covering 60 cities and five structure types. There are three basic steps. First, these data are screened

FIGURE 8. JHREMI Versus FRC Index: U.S. Office Market

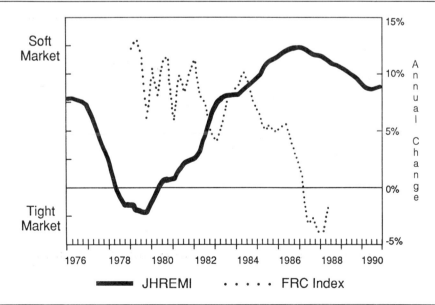

Source: John Hancock Properties Inc. Real Estate Research

constantly to see where we should be and when. Second, favorable markets are identified. Third, market timing strategies are implemented.

A big question concerns our ability to time the real estate markets. I believe it is possible to time the market, but only when one has information that no one else has and if one gets the information early enough. Timing is tricky because real estate is bulky, and it takes time to implement a strategy. We use market-timing strategies for acquisitions; obviously, we try to get in at the right time. For capital expenditures, we try to invest in a property with timely paybacks; for dispositions, we try to sell at the right time; and for asset management, we use it in such things as lease negotiations. It is helpful to our asset managers to have information on the future condition of a market before they try to negotiate a lease with a major tenant.

THE PORTFOLIO OPTIMIZATION PROCESS

The goal of portfolio optimization is to combine property types and locations to achieve superior portfolio performance—the greatest return for the least risk. The optimization process is long and complicated; it involves analyzing cities and property types. We analyze the basic economics and demographic influences affecting property types, as well as governing constraints. Next, we consider our strengths. Where do we know people? Where do we know deals? Where do our acquisition analysts and our management people have a leg up? We also try, with respect to separate account management, to be responsive to clients' preferences, which are often very strong and very clear.

The next step is to calculate the JHREMIs for location and property-type combinations, and to group similar markets to determine what places are substitutes for one another, from a portfolio perspective. The substitutes are not always within common regions: sometimes, Texas cities are grouped with Midwestern cities, and Florida cities with California cities. Then we forecast the JHREMIs to develop expected returns, forecasted standard deviations, and forecasted covariances. We do not rely on history. In the following examples, I have used historic variances and covariances, and Capital Asset Pricing Model expected returns. For actual portfolio construction, we forecast each of these numbers.

At this point it is possible to generate an efficient frontier, select the appropriate risk tolerance or return objective, and identify the optimal portfolio. We then invest in that portfolio, rebalancing the

portfolio as warranted. It is not a good idea to rebalance a portfolio so much that transaction costs consume return; in real estate that can happen because transactions are expensive. On the other hand, portfolios will not remain on the efficient frontier without rebalancing. Values change, which causes changes in the portfolio constraints, objectives, and expectations for the future.

The following two examples illustrate the output of the portfolio optimization process. The first example allocates by property type and the second allocates within a property type by urban area. Figure 9 shows an actual allocation exercise between warehouse, office, and retail properties. Portfolio A is the minimum risk portfolio. It is invested 23 percent in warehouse, 76 percent in retail, and not at all in office. This is not surprising to people familiar with the recent performance of the office market. As one moves toward the most risky position, the portfolio consists of 100 percent retail; there are no allocations to warehouse or office space. For comparison, I have plotted a "naive" portfolio—one with one-third in each category. Many people believe that the naive portfolio will be less risky because it is "diversified." But, will it be optimal? No, it will be light-years away from being optimal. The naive portfolio has significantly higher risk and lower return than the efficient portfolios. That is leaving money on the table—paying far too much for

FIGURE 9. Allocation by Property Type

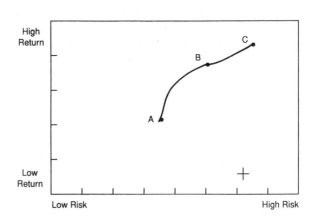

Portfolio Weights

	A	B	C	+
Warehouse	23.8%	5.7%	0.0%	33.3%
Office	0.0%	0.0%	0.0%	33.3%
Retail	76.1%	94.2%	100.0%	33.4%

Source: John Hancock Properties Inc. Real Estate Research

FIGURE 10. City Allocation Within Industrial Class

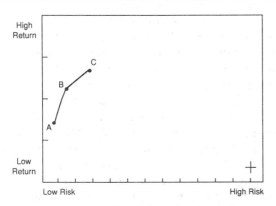

Portfolio Weights (%)

	A	B	C	+
Atlanta	0.0%	0.0%	0.0%	25.0%
Boston	21.4%	17.5%	7.1%	25.0%
Cincinnati	0.0%	0.0%	0.0%	25.0%
Washington	78.6%	82.5%	92.9%	25.0%

Source: John Hancock Properties Inc. Real Estate Research

what seems to be diversification.

The next example involves allocation by city within a property type—in this case, the industrial class. The allocation is between properties in four cities: Washington, Cincinnati, Boston, and Atlanta. Figure 10 shows three portfolios on the efficient frontier. The least risky portfolio has 21 percent invested in Boston and 78 percent invested in Washington. Washington has edged out Atlanta in this model because risk-adjusted yields are better in Washington. If one examines the correlation, however, the two cities behave very similarly. Therefore, if constraints prevented one from investing 78 percent in Washington properties, some of that allocation could be invested in Atlanta. That knowledge provides flexibility. The portfolio's returns will fall some, but the basic integrity and structure of the portfolio will be preserved. As one moves to a more risky position, the allocation to Washington increases and the allocation to Boston decreases, but Boston is never eliminated entirely. The model always wants a piece of Boston in the portfolio. A naively diversified portfolio, illustrated by the plus sign in the lower right corner, is once again significantly inferior.

CONCLUSION

To summarize, the ultimate goal in real estate investment is superior returns. There are two steps involved in achieving this goal. The first step is the careful purchase, management, and sale of individual properties; we believe that research leverages that process. The second step is meaningful and objective portfolio diversification, and without this, real estate investment is a time bomb. The design of real estate portfolios is dependent on good information, good data, and a way to identify good investments. In a manner analogous to the history of stock equity investing, real estate investors are beginning to take advantage of research and meaningful diversification.

Question and Answer Session

QUESTION: Please elaborate on the assumptions that you used to produce equilibrium returns.

KARNOSKY: Our equilibrium returns consist of three parts—a real rate that is consistent across all markets, an inflation premium, and a risk premium. The risk premium is the only one that will vary. The real rate of return is consistent with our estimates of global productivity, returns to factors of production, and so forth. There is a total global productivity constraint; we cannot receive more in real return than the global economy can produce. We have been operating with a trend inflation rate of 5 percent for several years. The risk premium is determined from analysis of the data; we try to detect regularities. We also compare risk premiums across markets to see if the risk premium in one market, which might in isolation look good, is consistent with risk premiums in other markets.

QUESTION: Referring to your data on the value of management, have you analyzed whether management detracts as much in other time periods as it did in the 10 years from 1974 to 1983?

KARNOSKY: We are currently running a model on the 10 years ending in 1987, for stocks, bonds, and cash. The total stock-bond selection process generates a positive return from 1977 to 1987. Market timing, actively shifting money around from asset class to asset class, remained negative. The total contribution of active management turned out to be, on balance, a small negative.

QUESTION: Has JHREMI been back-tested?

HUDSON-WILSON: We have examined the forecasting ability of JHREMI over approximately six years. The statistic has proven highly accurate over a 24-month period, and then the accuracy deteriorates. I think that the accuracy decreases mainly because the supply forecasts turn out to be less accurate than the demand forecasts.

QUESTION: With the change in the tax-reform environment, do you feel that the real estate market will be more demand-driven than supply-driven in the future?

HUDSON-WILSON: Yes, and I think that is good. I believe that markets will be more economically driven, and that both the demand and supply sides will have to work together more. The effect of mistakes are going to be felt much faster, because the tax benefit will not be there to soak up mistakes, and that is good for real estate markets.

QUESTION: It appears that you are more concerned with diversification by economic similarities of communities and underlying economic trends than by geographic region. Is it possible to diversify only on a geographic region basis, for example, Northeast, Midwest, and so forth?

HUDSON-WILSON: Absolutely not. And I would take it one step further. People who differentiate only on the demand side—on the economic characteristics of an area—will be wrong much of the time. Instead, people should look at the way the demand and supply sides interface over time. We are not buying an economic structure; we are buying a real estate market.

DESIGN OF REAL ESTATE PORTFOLIOS

Robert H. Zerbst

The design of real estate portfolios for institutional investors should be based on one's underlying beliefs about real estate and real estate markets. In this presentation, I would like to describe my firm's investment philosophy and outline how that philosophy affects our approach to designing real estate portfolios.

INVESTMENT PHILOSOPHY

Our investment philosophy is based on three basic beliefs about real estate. First, we believe that real estate is a local product, requiring local presence and local expertise to achieve above-average returns. Second, we believe that owner-managers who have an economic stake in the outcome of their decisions achieve superior returns over third-party managers. This proposition not only makes intuitive sense but has been validated empirically by studies utilizing institutional portfolios. We achieve local presence and expertise, as well as owner-management, through the use of joint ventures with local developers. We work with national developers who have local partners and regional developers who specialize in a particular area of the country. In all cases, they must have strong leasing and management capabilities and a long-term investment philosophy.

Third, we believe competition for well-located, fully leased properties in the United States is so intense that the yields have been bid down to the point where the returns are not commensurate with the attendant risk. In my opinion, shopping malls at 4 to 6 percent capitalization rates, office buildings at 6 to 8 percent capitalization rates, and industrial buildings at 7.5 to 8.5 percent capitalization rates do not provide sufficient yields to compensate for the risks undertaken. This is particularly true when reserve and capital line items are realistically considered in the yield analyses.

This three-part investment philosophy drives our approach to designing real estate portfolios. One of our goals is to increase our returns over those currently available in the market for quality properties. Given its management and marketplace, a property can only produce so much income and appreciation. In this environment, the principal way to increase returns is to lower the investment basis, or the cost, of the initial investment in the property. There are two basic techniques for lowering the basis of an investment, thereby increasing the returns. First, the investment should be initiated earlier in the real estate life cycle, and, second, financial structuring should be utilized.

INVESTMENT LIFE CYCLE

The life cycle of a real estate investment may be divided into four phases: (1) the raw land or predevelopment phase, (2) the construction phase, (3) the leasing phase, and (4) the operating phase. Later stages might include the sale or rehabilitation of the property, but these stages will not be considered here.

Risk and return expectations change with each phase of the real estate investment life cycle. Buying a property in the operating phase—that is, when it is already leased and occupied—is the least risky investment strategy. There are only two significant risks faced in this phase: (1) the likelihood that, and at what rate, the space can be re-leased when the tenants either default or their leases expire, and (2) whether increasing expenses may be controlled and recovered over time.

The earlier the phase in the life cycle, the greater the risk. For example, an investor in the leasing phase assumes the risk not only for the subsequent operating stage, but also for the risks associated with achieving pro forma rents and absorption for first generation leases. Similarly, an investor in the construction phase assumes additional risks—potential for design flaws, construction defects, strikes, interest-rate changes, or acts of God. The highest level of risk is associated with the predevelopment stage. Risks associated with the political process—e.g., zoning, entitlement approvals, and the time necessary to achieve them—must be factored into the analysis before investing at this stage.

It is important, no matter which life cycle stage one chooses, to understand the risk-return trade-offs of the investment. We have chosen to concentrate in the leasing phase. To be successful in underwriting lease-up risk requires thorough market research. In addition to examining the supply side, demand and the underlying factors driving demand must be analyzed.

To warrant investment, a real estate market typically must have several characteristics. The market—both the general market in the metropolitan area and the submarket in which the property is located—should be improving. An improving market is one in which vacancy rates are declining, concessions are declining, and effective rents are increasing. For example, we would rather make an investment in an office market with a 20 percent vacancy rate that is declining rapidly than in a market that is 10 percent vacant but moving in the opposite direction. Because vacancies tend to be disproportionately concentrated in ill-conceived or problem properties—except, of course, in such saturated areas as the Dallas, Houston, New Orleans, or Denver office markets—overall vacancy rates may be quite misleading. For example, it is quite possible to have good leasing success in submarkets with 20 percent vacancy where the property is in a good location, it appeals to the tenant in the particular market, and the development partner has an aggressive marketing organization and an existing tenant base. Investing in improving markets requires timing. Fortunately, markets do not move in unison but have different cycles. Therefore, investors must move constantly from market to market and city to city.

A final point on market timing should be emphasized. An investment is not complete and its returns are not realized until it is sold. Therefore, one should be very conscious of capital flows into real estate markets and invest only where there is liquidity for the asset and it is possible to see the exit.

FINANCIAL STRUCTURES

Investment in earlier phases of the property life cycle requires the assumption of higher risks to achieve higher expected returns. Another way to lower the basis of an investment and increase the return is to use financial structuring. Our firm uses participating mortgages and equity joint ventures as an alternative to direct equity purchase.

A participating mortgage is generally a first mortgage. It has a loan-to-value ratio of 80 to 90 percent, a coupon interest rate that is currently around 10 percent, and additional provisions providing for participation in the cash flows and residual value of the property. An equity joint venture is typically structured as a general partnership with a developer. The institution's equity may earn a cumulative preferred return and it has a percentage ownership interest in the cash flow and residual value of the property. Most of our joint ventures result in the institutions receiving 100 percent of the cash flow, at least in the early years of the investment, on a capital investment which is about 90 percent of the property's market value. We typically receive a 9 to 10 percent cumulative preference return on our investment, and then a participation in the remaining cash flow and residual value. The current yield in the early years is, therefore, higher than if we had bought the property outright. In most cases, having a lower basis in the investment also yields a higher holding period return than owning a 100 percent equity position does. Assuming third party management can match our partner's performance, there is a point at which the capital appreciation of the property is high enough that it would have been more attractive to have a 100 percent ownership. Generally, this situation only occurs if the property maintains an average annual appreciation rate of 8 to 12 percent over a 10-year holding period.

Financial structuring may also be used to manage the lease-up risk. For example, most of our transactions include an economic holdback, which means that we do not disburse to the partner or the borrower the full amount of the capital at closing. The partner earns a portion of the capital as he performs, that is, as he leases the property. We also use master leases, or some form of personal guarantee, during the lease-up period. The holdbacks and guarantees provide a cushion in cases where our pro forma rents and absorption projections were too optimistic. In general, deal structuring tends to shift a significant portion of the risk to development partners for those items where they have the expertise and responsibility.

The choice of financial structure provides additional flexibility to react to changing capital markets. Both a joint venture and a participating mortgage have two basic components: a fixed income, or coupon, and a participation in the upside potential. With a participating mortgage or an unleveraged joint venture, both of those components are combined in the same vehicle. The two components are separated in a leveraged joint venture. The fixed-income portion may be contributed by the same institution or it may come from a third party. The participation may be structured as debt or equity, but in any case the two components are separate. We choose the financial structure that maximizes the risk-adjusted yield on the funds we are managing. For example, when interest rates are high—more than 10 percent—a participating loan may be the best alternative. Alternatively, if interest rates are low—less than 10 percent—third-party guaranteed investment contract money may be the best alternative, allowing us to take advantage of the lower rates and leverage our returns.

The performance of structured financing is a function of several factors. First, the quality of the real estate is the most important factor, as it is with any equity investment. Good quality real estate that is well located and well designed is going to outperform other properties. In addition to the property, the quality of the joint venture partner and the deal structure are also crucial. Underwriting a real estate joint venture is analogous to underwriting a firm that has management in place, because one is investing not only in the asset itself, but in the management team that accompanies that asset. In addition, joint venture partners should be well capitalized. We try to avoid situations where a slight disruption in the partner's cash flow may affect their ability to perform on our projects. Further, partnerships should be with developers who have a track record, both in the property type and the locality. For example, even though we might do business with a development firm in Chicago, we will not typically invest in their first project in a new city, even if the project appears to have significant potential. Similarly, if a firm has been successful with apartments, we will not invest in a shopping center or an office building with them until they have demonstrated their ability to perform in that marketplace.

A good partnership structure is a delicate balance of incentives and controls. For example, the structure should be designed so that the partners make money only after the institution has made money, and when the property performs. Also, strong controls are necessary—for example, dilution provisions or buy-sell agreements—so that if the partner does not perform, the institution can take control of the partnership and the asset as soon as possible.

DESIGN OF A REAL ESTATE PORTFOLIO

There are several factors that must be considered in the design of real estate portfolios. The most significant factor is whether the institution is a corporation or a tax-exempt pension fund. Depreciation may be a drag on reported corporate earnings, but the major difference in structuring portfolios is that pension funds can recognize unrealized appreciation based on appraisal, but public corporations must sell an asset to recognize a gain. Our pension fund clients typically have three primary reasons for including real estate in their portfolio: (1) to increase stability of income; (2) to provide diversification; and (3) probably most importantly, to increase the real inflation-adjusted rate of return. Real estate investments offer opportunities to achieve all three of these goals.

For public corporations, the major objective is reportable earnings. Designing an inflation hedge or achieving long-term economic growth is a secondary goal. These investors cannot wait too long for that economic growth. Our corporate clients want a much shorter holding period, so that the gains may be recognized more quickly. Their investments include standby commitments, credit enhancements, rehabilitation property projects, retenanting projects, projects with significant lease-up risk, and projects that may be developed for sale. Once the value added is achieved, the property is sold to recognize the gain for reporting purposes.

The portfolio design must be consistent with the investor's goals. Different financial structures may be used to provide more flexibility in portfolio design and to achieve returns superior to those produced by simply buying the properties outright.

Alternative financial structures perform differently under different inflation scenarios. As examples, I will examine (1) fixed-rate loans, (2) participating loans, (3) 100 percent equity, and (4) leveraged equity. First, fixed-rate loans have constant nominal coupons, but their real return declines as inflation increases (see Figure 1). For example, a 10 percent interest rate and a 10 percent inflation rate result in zero real return over time. Second, participating loans with 50 percent participation, or kicker, will also have a declining real rate of return as inflation rates increase. The rate of decline is much slower than a fixed-rate loan because of the participation. Third, empirical studies have shown that institutional-grade properties in the United States have tended to track inflation over the long run. Thus, a 100 percent equity position in real estate should yield a constant real return around 6 percent. Finally, with a leveraged equity real estate investment, the real return increases as inflation goes up because of the fixed cost of the debt. The risk is obviously higher, as well.

The four structures have different real return

FIGURE 1. Expected Real Rates of Return (8/4/88)

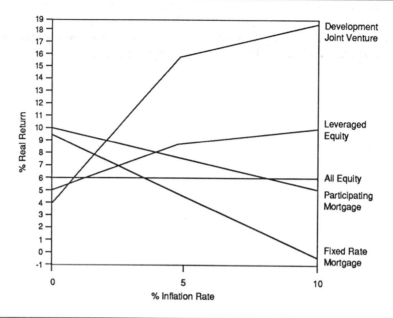

Source: Piedmont Realty Advisors

profiles. For example, the differences between a participating loan and an unleveraged equity purchase may be compared. The participating loan starts at a lower basis (e.g., 85 percent loan-to-value ratio) and has a coupon in excess of the applicable capitalization rate for the property. Therefore, it will have a higher current yield and a higher internal rate of return for most inflation scenarios than an all-equity purchase. If the average increase in the value of the property over a 10-year holding period is less than 8 percent, the increased value of the property will offset the lower basis and the higher coupon that gave the participating mortgage its initial advantage. The leveraged investment will also outperform the unleveraged investment for inflation rates that are 2 percent or more.

Many of our inflation-sensitive clients want a portfolio that yields a constant or hedged real return

FIGURE 2. Portfolio Design (8/4/88)

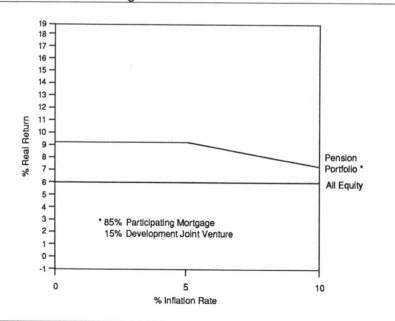

Source: Piedmont Realty Advisors

over different inflationary scenarios and a yield greater than that of an all-equity portfolio. One solution is to design a portfolio of 85 percent participating loans and 15 percent leveraged equity (see Figure 2). This portfolio will have the same amount of volatility and risk as an all-equity portfolio, but will produce higher yields over most inflation scenarios. Of course, these portfolios must also be diversified with regard to property types and geographic areas.

Management of Real Estate Portfolios

William T. Phillips

Stanford University has an endowment of about $1.6 billion. Of that endowment, approximately 16 percent, or about $250 million, has been allocated to real estate investments. This is quite an aggressive posture. Most university endowments consider allocations above 3 percent to be aggressive; a 5 or 10 percent allocation is very unusual. In this presentation, I will discuss the techniques for managing real estate portfolios, based on the decision-making process used at Stanford.

Before examining Stanford's experience, I must outline the environment within which these real estate decisions are being made. The university is located in the heart of the Silicon Valley—the Menlo Park-Palo Alto area of California—between San Francisco and San Jose. Real estate values in and around the university have been very strong in recent years. Office building rentals, for example, now average about $30 per square foot per annum, and office space can be built for $125 to $135 per square foot, all-inclusive. In San Francisco, by contrast, similar office space would probably cost about $250-$300 per square foot to build, and rents would not be substantially higher. The wealth of value around Stanford with respect to all types of real estate is quite enormous.

Stanford's relatively large allocation to real estate is a function of the university's investment philosophy for its endowment. That philosophy is based on the perception that educational institutions have some unique problems in terms of competitiveness and growth in the future. At Stanford, the treasurer's office believes that the university's performance and growth depend on the endowment achieving higher-than-average returns. The additional money earned can then provide lower tuition, better facilities, and better research. We hope that this will lead to a better faculty, better students, and a highly competitive school.

Stanford's investment philosophy is also heavily influenced by the fact that it owns approximately 8,500 acres of land including and surrounding the campus. This situation presents an interesting investment problem: the university cannot use all of that land for academic purposes, at least at present,

but the endowment stipulates that the land cannot be sold. The land may be leased, however, and there is no restriction on the length of leases. Thus, in reality, the limitations on the land's use are not severe. In fact, we have developed a major research park, a major shopping center, and a number of commercial developments in the area surrounding the university. Most of the land, including the research park, is still reserved for academic purposes in the future. The shopping center is considered part of the university's investment pool in real estate.

Stanford's investment objective for the endowment fund is to achieve a 6.75 percent real return per year, with diversification and minimum volatility. This objective allows the university not only to maintain the real value of its endowment funds, but also to grow by 2 percent per year. Further, the endowment fund is expected to support a consistent proportion of the university's operating budget. To meet these investment objectives, the endowment fund's investment performance must be superior to that of most other endowments.

Stanford's superior performance in recent years has been largely attributable to the university's approach to portfolio diversification and its appreciation of the importance of nontraditional assets, such as real estate, venture capital, and international equities. Within Stanford's investment strategy, the allocation to the real estate block has been particularly important.

Figure 1 shows the effect of diversification on a portfolio's risk-return potential. The 60/40 stock/bond curve does not meet our 6.75 percent total real return requirement. Adding real estate to the portfolio reduces the risk of the portfolio and provides a higher return. (We do not believe that the historic volatility figure for real estate is an accurate reflection of risk, so we use a higher estimate of risk in our optimization models.) The figure also shows what happens when other equity classes are added. The investment return and volatility performance of a portfolio with seven asset classes are shown in Table 1. Over the past five years, the multiasset portfolio has achieved a compound return that is similar to the S&P 500, but without its volatility.

FIGURE 1. Improvement in Risk-Return Trade-off

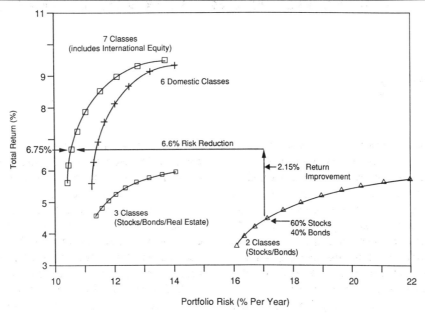

Source: Stanford University Treasurer's Office

THE REAL ESTATE PORTFOLIO

Stanford's real estate investment program has two parts. First, we would like to provide housing assistance to Stanford faculty. The real estate environment in the Palo Alto area entails not only a high cost for office, retail, R&D, and warehouse space, but also for residential properties. Houses costing $1 million are common, presenting problems for a university. Faculty may initially be attracted to Stanford by superior salaries, but later they may be discouraged by the difficulty of finding affordable housing. Stanford offers two alternatives to its faculty: (1) it offers rental housing on campus, and (2) it provides money for second-mortgage financing. Through the second-mortgage program, faculty may obtain financing at low interest rates by giving up a large share of the property appreciation. Initially, these mortgage programs were very attractive, but recent participation in the programs has diminished, primarily because giving up the appreciation is probably too much to pay for low-interest-rate financing. Thus, although the program is still necessary for many of the faculty coming to Palo Alto, I think its decline will continue as housing prices rise.

The second part of our real estate investment program involves direct equity positions in real estate. The purpose of the equity-based real estate portfolio within the total endowment is to provide appropriate diversification and to hedge the endowment by providing high cash-on-cash yield,

protection against unanticipated inflation, and a negative correlation to equities and fixed-income securities. To achieve this purpose, four investment goals were established: (1) realize a 7 percent real rate of return, (2) keep pace with inflation, (3) develop durable partnership arrangements, and (4) diversify away from the Stanford-Silicon Valley-Bay area.

The goal of a 7 percent real rate of return requires us to be very aggressive in the real estate investments we make. Value-added is not only something we hope for, it is something that must be built into the return performance of all real estate investments.

Second, an investment's inflation protection must be in force throughout the entire period that we hold that piece of real estate. We cannot afford to invest

TABLE 1. Portfolio Performance: Annualized Results for the Five Years Ended 6/30/88

	Merged Pools	S&P 500
Compound return	14.6%	14.6%
Volatility	10.5%	18.8%
Return per unit of volatility	1.5x	0.8x

Source: Stanford University Treasurer's Office

FIGURE 2.   Stanford University Composition by Property Type

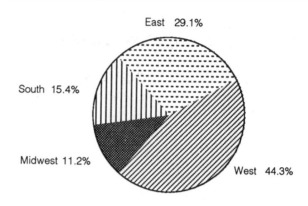

Office 24%

Residential 4.2%

Land 15.1%

Hotel/Motel 0.8%

R & D 7.2%

Industrial 21%

Retail 27.7%

Without Stanford Shopping Center (6/30/88)

FIGURE 3.   Stanford University Composition by Property Location

East 29.1%

South 15.4%

Midwest 11.2%

West 44.3%

Without Stanford Shopping Center (6/30/88)

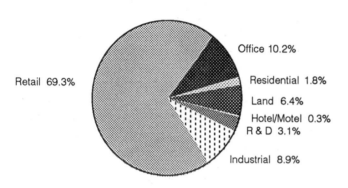

Retail 69.3%

Office 10.2%

Residential 1.8%

Land 6.4%

Hotel/Motel 0.3%

R & D 3.1%

Industrial 8.9%

With Stanford Shopping Center (6/30/88)

Source: Institutional Property Consultants, Inc.

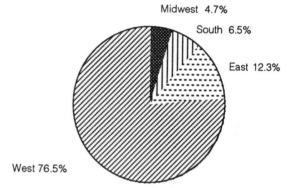

Midwest 4.7%

South 6.5%

East 12.3%

West 76.5%

With Stanford Shopping Center (6/30/88)

Source: Institutional Property Consultants, Inc.

in an attractive retail property, for example a shopping center, that has space under lease with a cap on inflation-adjusted rents.

Third, we must develop enduring partnerships with knowledgeable real estate people.

The fourth investment goal is to diversify away from the Bay area. We are not unaware that our great

real estate market is in an earthquake-prone area and that our success results partly from our location in an area supported by high-tech industry. We know that if the high-tech industry fails, the return on our real estate portfolio will be affected. Also, if an earthquake hits Palo Alto, it will affect the university, the shopping center, the research park, and a sub-

TABLE 2. Stanford University Real Estate Investment Returns

	1983	1984	1985	1986	1987	5-year average
Without Stanford Shopping Center	11.8%	14.2%	14.7%	10.6%	5.8%	11.4%
With Stanford Shopping Center	11.7%	30.6%	22.5%	12.2%	32.0%	21.5%

Source: Stanford University

FIGURE 4. Stanford University Composition by
Life Cycle Stage

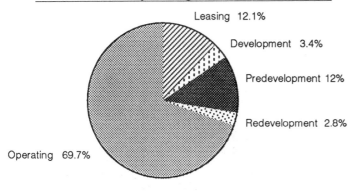

Leasing 12.1%

Development 3.4%

Predevelopment 12%

Redevelopment 2.8%

Operating 69.7%

Without Stanford Shopping Center (6/30/88)

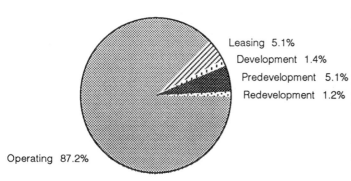

Leasing 5.1%

Development 1.4%

Predevelopment 5.1%

Redevelopment 1.2%

Operating 87.2%

With Stanford Shopping Center (6/30/88)

Source: Institutional Property Consultants, Inc.

stantial portion of our other real estate investments. We cannot let such events harm Stanford's ability to compete as a first-rate university.

DIVERSIFICATION IN THE REAL ESTATE PORTFOLIO

The real estate program started with the Stanford Shopping Center as its primary element. That shopping center now represents slightly less than half of the total real estate investments. To evaluate the success of our real estate program, it is important to separate the shopping center from the other investments, in part because the shopping center reflects what may be a peculiar phenomenon of the time—that the income and value of retail properties, especially regional shopping centers, have increased

so much in the past several years that it is hard to believe the performance will continue during the next 10 years.

Table 2 shows the return on the real estate portfolio from 1983 to 1987. The performance of the Stanford Shopping Center is related to the way we value it. We started by capping its income at 9 percent. We have, during this period, reduced that cap rate incrementally, but only to the 8 percent level. Thus, we are not carrying the shopping center at current value. The returns attributed to the shopping center are not a result of the dramatic drop in cap rates from, say, the 9 percent level to the approximately 4.5 percent level that is probably appropriate for a shopping center of Stanford's quality. Instead, the returns are basically the result of income and sales growth at the shopping center.

The diversification of the real estate portfolio is illustrated in Figures 2 through 4. Figure 2 shows the portfolio composition by property type. If we were diversifying properly, starting with Stanford Shopping Center as the basis for the portfolio, the composition excluding the shopping center should be very light on retail, but it is not; the endowment is invested more heavily in retail than in any other property type. The composition resembles that of other real estate portfolios attempting to reap the benefits of the current real estate market—office properties are underperforming, retail properties are overperforming, and interest in land and in industrial properties is increasing.

Figure 3 shows the portfolio's diversification by property location over geographic areas. Once again, the portfolio is not well diversified. We should be underemphasizing the Western region and overemphasizing the others. Nevertheless, the West represents a significant percentage within the portfolio.

Figure 4 shows diversification by life cycle stage. As we move into a market that has seen declining capitalization rates, we should be moving more and more into development property and away from operating properties like the Stanford Shopping Center. Nevertheless, we still show an extremely heavy emphasis on operating properties, although, for a major institution, the investment of almost one third of the balance of the portfolio in some level of development—from predevelopment through leasing—is quite high and quite aggressive. This has helped the portfolio achieve the kind of real return we seek.

There are three basic reasons why we have not been successful in our attempts at diversification. First, the market condition has a major influence on what may be bought in the real estate market. We may want to get away from shopping centers and go more heavily into opportunistic office and land assemblages, for example, but those opportunities simply are not available when that area of the market is suffering. Given the array of investments in the recent market, then, the best opportunities in many cases have been in the retail area. Many of these opportunities have been on the West Coast, and particularly in the Los Angeles area, and many have been in operating properties that needed some management turnaround to make them more successful investments.

Second, competitive conditions have affected our strategy. We have not invested heavily in regional shopping centers, although we have invested more in retail, simply because competition for that type of real estate asset has been heavy.

Third, the dynamics of real estate performance are particularly important in determining what to invest in. The developers and owner-investors of property we want to be associated with are good at their job partly because of their knowledge of local markets. Often because of these relations, investors remain in the real estate and geographic areas in which their contacts operate, despite the expressed desire to diversify out of those areas.

Question and Answer Session

QUESTION: Please provide some examples of the returns from the four segments of the real estate life cycle that you described.

ZERBST: For completed, fully leased properties, the initial cash return is typically in the 7 to 9 percent range and the internal rate of return (IRR) in the 10.5 to 12.0 percent range, assuming 5 percent inflation. In the lease-up phase, the rates would depend on the degree of leasing. Generally, the initial stabilized returns would be in the range of 9 to 10 percent, with an IRR in the range of 12.5 to 14 percent. In the predevelopment phase, the yield would probably be 500 to 800 basis points higher.

QUESTION: In your presentation, you indicated that the operating cycle phase is over-valued. Do you think that the risk is higher today in the lease-up phase than it would be otherwise?

ZERBST: Yes, in general that is true. There is more risk in the lease-up phase in today's market environment for several reasons: (1) most markets are overbuilt, (2) tenants and investors are uncertain whether there is going to be a slowdown in the overall economy, and (3) most experts think that real estate space, particularly office space, will not be absorbed as fast in the future as it was absorbed in the past. If markets, partners, and properties are chosen carefully, however, higher returns should compensate for the added risk.

QUESTION: What is the typical length of time for a shared appreciation mortgage?

ZERBST: The average participating mortgage term is probably 10 years. Some mortgages have much longer terms—up to 17- or 18-year lock-in terms. At the other end of the spectrum, some mortgages have a 10- or 20-year term, but with a call provision that allows the lender to call the loan in as few as five years. Usually the lock-in provision and the call date are established based on an estimate of the full leasing cycle for a property. This way the lender realizes the value enhancement before the mortgage can be repaid.

QUESTION: Is there a relation between the term of the participating mortgage and the length of time deemed necessary to maximize the property value?

ZERBST: Yes. Lenders do not want to be taken out of an investment before the property has had a chance to maximize its value. On the other hand, the borrower wants to make sure the investment is financed "permanently." If the loan could be called in in a relatively short period of time, say three years, the financing would probably not appeal to the borrower.

QUESTION: Please describe how your development partners are compensated.

ZERBST: Generally, development partners earn an overhead fee and a small profit percentage for developing the property. They also receive leasing commissions and property management fees. Their primary incentive, or at least it should be, is their percentage interest in the property's cash flow and appreciation.

QUESTION: What factors do you look at to determine which markets to get into, and when to get into them?

ZERBST: Aside from the markets that are a total loss, there are good deals and bad deals in every market. The return depends on what one pays for a property. It is possible to realize disappointing returns in a strong market because you paid too high a price for the property, and it is possible to realize a great return in a weaker market through a good deal or a good structure. We look for markets that are moving in the right direction. For example, last year we made some investments in Portland, Oregon which had not had absorption and had experienced very slow growth for a long time. The project was an office building in the suburbs that was about 33 percent vacant, but it was clear that things were turning around. In that area, there was no more new construction and there was strong absorption, and we had a property that we felt would attract both suburban tenants and tenants from downtown.

QUESTION: Are the real estate volatility measures adequate in your opinion?

PHILLIPS: That is a hard question. We know that the volatility attributed to real estate, at levels of 2 to 4 percent, is completely unrealistic. It is almost impossible, however, to calculate what that volatility would be if real estate were traded every day. Real estate volatility is fairly low because it is based on appraised values. In many cases, however, appraised values are a self-fulfilling prophecy; often, property owners will not sell their real estate at values that represent a considerable discount to the appraised values. Thus, real estate values tend to reflect the optimist, not the pessimist in the market. But if that is the market, then these lower volatility levels do reflect some truth.

QUESTION: Based on the diversification of your investments, it would appear that you believe that the risk of an earthquake affecting both the Bay area and the Los Angeles metroplex is relatively low. Is that true?

PHILLIPS: The risk is actually surprisingly low. Both Stanford and Berkeley have done a number of studies on the earthquake situation. The results of simulation models indicate that if an earthquake of the magnitude that San Francisco had in 1906 occurred along one of the major fault lines, the Stanford campus would experience a 6 to 10 percent loss of total building value.

Measurement of the Performance of Real Estate

Barbara R. Cambon

Many aspects of measuring real estate performance have not yet been addressed by the real estate industry. For example, some of the performance measures that have been applied to financial instruments are not necessarily appropriate for measuring real estate investment performance. First, there is the basic pricing mechanism that applies to the different asset classes: Stocks and bonds enjoy daily marking to market, whereas real estate is dependent on the appraisal process, with all the inherent difficulties caused by different frequencies of appraisals and the imprecision of the appraisal process itself. A second factor is the cash flow part of investment performance: Stocks and bonds generate dividends and interest payments, but in real estate one must consider property-level income, property-level net cash flow, and cash distributions out of the investment. A third factor is the availability and timing of investments in the real estate sector. The time that is required to locate a property, work through all the due diligence, and ultimately make an investment may be considerable, and is generally measured in months instead of days. A final consideration is the "lumpiness" of the real estate investment—the large amount of money required to go into a unique asset that only a single investor may acquire.

METHODS OF PERFORMANCE MEASUREMENT

Several different performance measurement methods are used today, primarily by three groups: pension plan sponsors, their consultants, and the real estate investment management firms that provide acquisition and asset management services to major tax-exempt investors.

Performance measurement techniques have evolved over time. In the 1960s, the Bank Administration Institute undertook a study to develop a methodology for evaluating the performance of mutual funds. The study focused on stock and bond funds, because no real estate commingled funds existed at that time; the first real estate fund started in the early 1970s. This study set a time-weighted rate-of-return methodology as the standard for performance measurement for mutual funds.

In the 1970s, real estate investment management firms grew and real estate gained greater acceptance as an asset class for institutional investors. For these reasons, it became necessary to create a performance index solely for real estate. A group of real estate investment management firms formed the National Council of Real Estate Investment Fiduciaries (NCREIF) which sponsors an index widely used to discuss the performance of real estate investments exclusively for institutional investors. The index started in 1978 and, therefore, tracks only 10 years of performance—a short period relative to most financial assets. The NCREIF index focuses on the aggregate performance of individual property investments and the income generated by those investments. It also measures changes in the value of the properties from period to period. This index has become widely accepted as a performance benchmark for institutional equity real estate investments.

Another performance measure is an index that tracks the performance of commingled funds for real estate. To evaluate, identify, and select commingled funds, pension plan sponsors and their consultants wanted to compare the historical performance at the fund level, not the property level. Out of that need arose a database of real estate commingled fund performance.

A fourth measure of performance focuses on the investor's investment performance. This method measures the performance of the dollars allocated to real estate, focusing on the cash contributions to real estate and the distributions of cash flow from real estate investments. Establishing the historical record of investors' individual real estate investments and their total portfolio performance permits evaluation of their portfolios by relating performance to portfolio objectives.

RATE OF RETURN CALCULATIONS FOR REAL ESTATE

The various methods of measuring the performance of real estate portfolios attempt to determine the income generated by the portfolio, the change in the market value of the real estate, and the total rate of return—both the income and the appreciation components—on a periodic basis. In real estate, performance is generally measured on a quarterly basis. I use the term "real estate portfolios" generically to include both open-end and closed-end funds, as well as separately managed accounts comprising a number of real estate properties.

There are two basic types of returns: performance returns and expected returns. Performance returns measure the actual historical experience of an investment; these rates of return could be either time-weighted or dollar-weighted. Expected returns are used to compare different investment alternatives and evaluate the prospective performance of the investment; this rate of return is typically dollar-weighted.

There are four basic single-period measures of return: cash-on-cash yield, capitalization rate, income return, and appreciation return. Cash-on-cash yields are calculated as the cash distributed to the investor divided by the original cash investment, as shown in Table 1. For example, an investment with an original cash price of $1,000 and a cash distribution of $70 would have a cash-on-cash yield of 7 percent ($70/$1,000). Typically, cash-on-cash yields are used to measure performance at the property investment level. Cash-on-cash yields may take into account not only the original cash investment, but also any additional capital contributions into the investment during the period.

Another single-period measure is the capitalization rate. Capitalization rates are probably the most frequently discussed measures of a property's performance. Capitalization rates are defined as the existing annual net operating income, divided by the transaction price, as shown in Table 2. For example, a transaction price of $150 million and in-place cash flow of $9 million equates to a capitalization rate of 6 percent. Capitalization rates are basically the inverse of the price/earnings ratio. Again, these measures are not portfolio-level measures, they are generally used at the property level.

Historically, capitalization rates have been in the range of 9 to 10 percent; current rates for prime properties are now as low as 5 to 7 percent. These rates serve as indicators of supply and demand in the marketplace. For example, capitalization rates for major regional shopping centers are approximately

TABLE 1. Calculation of Cash-On-Cash Yield

Formula:

$$\text{Yield} = \frac{\text{Cash Distributed}}{\text{Original Cash Investment}}$$

Example:

Original Cost	$1,000
Cash Distributed	$ 70
Yield	7 percent

Source: Institutional Property Consultants, Inc.

5 to 6 percent, indicating a very strong demand for that particular property subtype in today's marketplace. Major office buildings in the largest cities in the United States—primarily New York, Chicago, and Los Angeles—are also selling at capitalization rates in the 6 percent range; this rate indicates the demand for that type of property.

The income return methodology measures the income return on a property. The income in this calculation does not refer to dividend distributions or interest payments; rather, it refers to the income earned at the property level. Because of the various accounting methodologies used in the real estate industry, there is considerable debate over the appropriate way to calculate this measure. Typically, this method does not provide a pure cash flow accounting number. A number of accounting considerations may have a significant impact on the calculation of income earned in real estate, including whether depreciation is taken into account, how various items are amortized, and whether major capital expenditures, tenant improvements, or leasing commissions made on a property are immediately expensed, capitalized, or capitalized and amortized.

The income return measure is affected by the choice of the investment base; it may be calculated

TABLE 2. Calculation of Capitalization Rate

Formula:

$$\text{Capitalization Ratio} = \frac{\text{Net Operating Income}}{\text{Transaction Price}}$$

Example:

Transaction Price	$150,000
Net Operating Income	$ 9,000
Capitalization Rate	6 percent

Source: Institutional Property Consultants, Inc.

TABLE 3. Calculation of Income Return

Formula:

Income Return/Cost = $\dfrac{\text{Current Income}}{\text{Cost}}$

or

Income Return/Market = $\dfrac{\text{Current Income}}{\text{Market Value}}$

Example:

Original Cost	$1,000
Market Value	$1,200
Current Income	$ 85 per year
Income Return/Cost =	8.5 percent
Income Return/Market =	7.1 percent

Source: Institutional Property Consultants, Inc.

using the original cost of the investment or the current market value of the investment, as shown in Table 3. For example, an investment with an original cost of $1,000, a current market value of $1,200, and current income of $85, would have an income return on cost of 8.5 percent and an income return on market value of 7.1 percent. This measure of performance may also be affected by a manager's decision to distribute or retain cash, and the timing of the cash flows into and out of the investment.

The fourth single-period measure is the appreciation return. The purpose of the appreciation return is to measure the change in the market value of the property or the portfolio during the period. This measure is designed to take into account realized gains and losses from transactions, as well as unrealized gains or losses which result from appraisals conducted during the period. The formula for the appreciation return is shown in Table 4. Appreciation returns are affected by capital additions to the market value that occur during the period for which the appreciation is being measured, and how those interperiod capital flows are accounted for.

Interperiod cash flows may be taken into consideration in several ways. First, a midperiod convention may be used for capital additions, a method which assumes that the capital addition occurs in the middle of the period. Second, interperiod movements may be accounted for using a dollar-day weighting technique, which captures the effect of changes in the investment base on the actual day that it occurred.

In addition to single-period measures of performance, investors and investment managers use two holding-period returns: a time-weighted rate of return and a dollar-weighted rate of return. The time-weighted rate of return is defined as a series of periodic returns that are linked together, where the period is the shortest interval for which information is available. In real estate, the quarterly interval has evolved as the standard for measuring time-weighted rates of return. Although the validity of this period is arguable, it has become the standard for our industry.

Time-weighted rates of return are calculated using total rates of return for the period. The basic formula is shown in Table 5. This methodology may also be used for multiple-year periods with one modification: the product of the subperiod returns must be adjusted to annualize the return. For example, the annualized return for eight quarters would be the square root of the product of one plus the quarterly returns.

The dollar-weighted rate of return is intended to measure the return per unit of invested assets. The basic dollar-weighted rate-of-return calculation is an internal rate of return formula that solves for the rate which, when used to discount all of the cash flows during the period, makes the net present value equal to zero. The one major difference in real estate is that, for purposes of calculating a historical dollar-weighted rate of return for assets currently held in a portfolio, a residual value that is equal to the ending

TABLE 4. Calculation of Appreciation Return

Formula:

Appreciation Return = $\dfrac{\text{Ending Mkt Value - Beginning Mkt Value}}{\text{Beginning Mkt Value}}$

Example:

Ending Market Value	$1,200	
Beginning Market Value	$1,000	
Return =		20 percent

Source: Institutional Property Consultants, Inc.

market value of the investments is used.

TECHNIQUES FOR MEASURING PERFORMANCE

The most common technique used by real estate investment managers to measure and report investment performance is the time-weighted rate of return. This is a performance return because it evaluates the actual, historical results generated by an investment. A time-weighted rate of return measures the performance of the manager of a fund; it does not consider the timing of major cash flows between the investor and the manager. In fact, it neutralizes the impact of the investor's allocation and timing decisions. Time-weighted rates of return have become the most appropriate measures for comparative performance evaluations for real estate managers because they measure the impact of the manager's investment decisions.

Time-weighted rate-of-return calculations work very well when applied to the total rate of return. They do not work well when applied to the components of return, however. This may be a major problem. There is no standard for calculating time-weighted rates of return on a consistent basis. In fact, the NCREIF recently conducted a study of different methodologies used by investment managers to calculate and report income and appreciation components to their investors. I was concerned by the study's findings. The following are a few examples of methods that various managers reported using to calculate income and appreciation components of return:

(1) time-weight both the annual income returns and the annual total returns, and then take the difference between the two as the appreciation number;

(2) time-weight both the annual appreciation returns and the total returns, and then plug in the income number;

(3) time-weight the appreciation returns, the income returns, and the total return, and prorate the components so that they sum to the total return;

(4) assume that the income and appreciation returns do not need to equal the total return, and, therefore, no mathematical formula or proration is necessary. Mathematically, the numbers did not correspond; the sum of the income and appreciation returns was not the same as the total return, and did not need to be.

Needless to say, none of these methods is terribly satisfying to an investor trying to evaluate a manager's strategy, whether it is an income-generating strategy or a value-added strategy. The industry is trying to determine an acceptable methodology for the calculation of the components of return so that the dollars ultimately add up to the total return when the income generated by the investment is separated from the change in value.

The most widely accepted performance measurement technique for most individual investments is a dollar-weighted or internal rate-of-return calculation method. Dollar-weighted rates of return are not used by real estate managers to report performance to investors or to report the performance of portfolios or funds to investors. They are primarily used to measure the prospective investment performance of a single property. Dollar-weighted rates of return measure the impact of both the timing and the magnitude of investor contributions when used on a historical basis. Ultimately, a historical internal rate of return or dollar-weighted rate of return for an investor's entire portfolio will show the impact of the asset allocation

---

TABLE 5. Time-Weighted Rate of Return

Formula:
1-year Return	=	$[[(1+R_{Q1})(1+R_{Q2})(1+R_{Q3})(1+R_{Q4})]-1] \times 100$
Multi-year Return	=	$[[(1+R_{Q1})(1+R_{Q2})...(1+R_{Qn})]^{1/n}-1] \times (100)$
		where n = number of years

Example:
Return Q_1	2.1%
Return Q_2	1.8%
Return Q_3	2.7%
Return Q_4	1.5%
1-Year Return	= $[[(1.021)(1.018)(1.027)(1.015)]-1] \times 100$
	= 8.35%

Source: Institutional Property Consultants, Inc.

decisions made by the investor.

The dollar-weighted return is a performance return, because it may be used to capture actual, historical investment returns. The dollar-weighted return is also an expected return, because it considers the anticipated return on an investor's position in making that investment allocation decision. Dollar-weighted rates of return take into account the timing of the major cash flows into and out of an investment.

The difference between a time-weighted rate of return and a dollar-weighted rate of return is illustrated in Table 6. At the beginning of year one, the investor bought one unit worth $1,000. At the end of year one, the unit was worth $900. The investor then bought an additional unit for $900. At the end of year two, one unit was worth $1,080. The return in the first year was -10 percent; the return in the second year was 20 percent. The time-weighted return was 3.92 percent, determined by calculating the rates for the two individual periods, linking them together, and then annualizing that rate. Because the investor was smart enough to have most of his or her dollars invested during the second year of this holding period, the dollar-weighted rate of return was 8.7 percent.

CONCLUSION

One of the problems with developing reliable and consistent performance measurement in the real estate industry is getting all investment managers to use the same formula. Examples of some simple and straightforward formulas are provided in this presentation, but many issues related to the timing and treatment of cash flows during the holding period are treated inconsistently within the real estate industry. One of these issues is how people calculate income or account for income calculated on an effective rent basis. Some investors believe that it is most appropriate to report income by taking the entire income over the term of a lease for a property, and including a portion of that income in each reporting period during that lease term. Thus, on an effective rent basis, income returns that occur early

TABLE 6. Rate of Return Example

Begin Year 1 :	1 unit =	$1,000
End Year 1 :	1 unit =	$900
End Year 1 :	+ 1 unit @	$900
End Year 2 :	1 unit =	$1,080
Return Year 1 :		-10%
Return Year 2 :		+20%
Time-Weighted Return :		3.92%
Dollar-Weighted Return :		8.70%

Source: Institutional Property Consultants, Inc.

in the holding period of an investment may be substantially higher than the actual cash flow from the property, particularly in those markets where major rental concessions are being given and, in fact, little or no cash flow may be coming in from that investment. An additional risk in using the effective rent calculation is that, at the end of a free-rent period, the tenant may elect to move out, and the property owner may never realize the rental income which had been accrued over the lease term. Such distortions in the treatment of income at the accounting level have a major impact on performance measures.

A second problem that must be resolved is the inconsistency in the calculation of the return components. As our industry has grown—and it is still a relatively young industry—managers have undertaken a wider range of investment strategies, some focusing on income and some focusing on appreciation. The results of these efforts will ultimately show in the performance they report, but it will be difficult to differentiate between the income and appreciation components of performance.

The third problem that the industry faces is its appraisal data. Full-cycle returns in the real estate industry have been lacking to date because there have not been very many property sales upon which to calculate full-cycle holding period returns. We must work toward consistent definitions and calculations for income and for appreciation, so that investors can make performance comparisons.

Question and Answer Session

QUESTION: What is unique about measuring real estate fund performance versus the performance of other securities?

CAMBON: The biggest difference is the source of market value data. Investors cannot obtain a daily market price for real estate. Generally, the frequency of property appraisals is annual, so investors must draw conclusions from quarterly measures of return and annual appraisal cycles. Other differences relate to the timing of events in real estate that may vary significantly from the activity in a financial instrument. Bonds have a very regular schedule of cash flows, which influences how the bonds are valued. In real estate, the net cash flows may be at different and far less certain intervals, although the lease payments should be fairly consistent. Because of the irregular pattern, people have developed different conventions to account for these interperiod cash flows. For example, some people assume that a third of the total income for the quarter leaves the fund or the property each month to facilitate calculations.

QUESTION: Is there a time-weighted rate of return that is appropriate for measuring the performance of real estate managers who determine the amounts and timing of cash flows in and out of the invested part of the fund?

CAMBON: No distinction is made between closed-end funds and open-end funds when time-weighted rates of return are calculated. The implicit assumption in a time-weighted rate-of-return calculation is that all cash flows are reinvested. Thus, if the time-weighted rate of return were to account for the regular cash distribution in a closed-end fund, property performance being equal, closed-end funds would have lower rates of return than open-end funds. Again, the purpose of the time-weighted rate of return is to allow for meaningful performance comparisons among managers and funds, without regard to dollar amounts and without regard to the structure of the fund itself. The goal is to make meaningful performance comparisons and to ensure that the methodology itself neutralizes the impact of cash distributions from a closed-end fund.

Self-Evaluation Examination

1. The size of the domestic commercial real estate market is:

    a)   Comparable to the U.S. bond market.
    b)   Comparable to the U.S. common stock market.
    c)   Comparable to the U.S. venture capital market.
    d)   Comparable to the global common stock market.

2. Worldwide, the value of U.S. commercial real estate is:

    a)   Comparable to the value of all bond markets.
    b)   Comparable to the value of all common stock markets.
    c)   Greater than the value of all common stock markets.
    d)   The value cannot be calculated.

3. According to Lillard, which of the following is a reason for investing in real estate?

    a)   Real estate provides high risk-adjusted returns.
    b)   Real estate provides low volatility.
    c)   Real estate provides protection against inflation.
    d)   All of the above.

4. According to Lillard, which of the following is a reason for *not* investing in real estate?

    a)   Real estate is less marketable than other securities.
    b)   There are less historical data available for real estate.
    c)   Volatility is believed to be greater than valuation methods imply.
    d)   All of the above.

5. The Japanese own more U.S. property than any other country.

    a)   True.
    b)   False.

6. The key to economic value in real estate is:

    a)   The demand for space by users.
    b)   The availability of substitute space.
    c)   A function of the rental income available from the space.
    d)   The demand for rental income by investors.

7. The definition of the market value of real estate is:

    a)   The value of the property to an institutional investor.
    b)   The appraised value of the property.
    c)   The value of the property to a typical investor.
    d)   The going-concern value of the property.

8. According to Fisher, the real estate markets are as efficient as the stock market.

   a) True.
   b) False.

9. All of the following statements characterize real estate *except:*

   a) Real estate is valued using an auction market.
   b) Landmark buildings are not followed by a cadre of Wall Street analysts.
   c) Information on real estate is not widely disseminated.
   d) The trading frequency of real estate properties is very low.

10. According to McMillan, the correlation statistic is free of the problems that make the standard deviation of returns statistic meaningless for real estate.

    a) True.
    b) False.

11. According to Oliver, all of the following are reasons to invest in publicly traded real estate securities *except:*

    a) Real estate securities are hybrid securities whose performance is similar to both equities and direct ownership.
    b) Many real estate securities sell at relatively high yields.
    c) There is a good source of information on real estate securities.
    d) Real estate securities offer both product and geographic diversification.

12. According to Karnosky, the highest historical correlation is between real estate and:

    a) U.S. equity.
    b) Domestic bonds.
    c) Non-U.S. equity.
    d) Nondollar bonds.

13. According to Karnosky, active management in the selection of specific stocks and bonds:

    a) Decreased the average portfolio return.
    b) Increased the average portfolio return.
    c) Had no significant effect on the average portfolio return.
    d) It was not possible to measure the effect.

14. From a portfolio manager's perspective, the key to real estate investing is to make a decision on a property within a real estate portfolio context, and then within a portfolio context relative to all other assets that are held.

    a) True.
    b) False.

15. The foundation of both individual investments and portfolio design is:

    a) Project analysis.
    b) Risk analysis.
    c) Real estate research.
    d) Correlation analysis.

16. Hudson-Wilson recommends basing real estate decisions on a thorough analysis of the historical data.

    a) True.
    b) False.

17. The life cycle of real estate investment includes all of the following stages *except:*

    a) The leasing phase.
    b) The operating phase.
    c) The predevelopment phase.
    d) The mature phase.

18. Investments in earlier phases of the life cycle of real estate investment requires the assumption of higher risks to achieve higher expected returns.

    a) True.
    b) False.

19. According to Phillips, all of the following reasons interfered with Stanford's attempts to diversify its real estate portfolio *except:*

    a) Market conditions.
    b) Competitive conditions.
    c) Concern about earthquake damage.
    d) Partnership relations in geographic regions.

20. The performance measures that have been applied to financial instruments are equally appropriate for measuring the performance of real estate investment performance.

    a) True.
    b) False.

Self-Evaluation Answers

See Maginn:
    1. b   Both have an estimated market value in the mid-$3 trillion range.
    2. c

See Lillard:
    3. d   All of the above.
    4. d   All of the above.
    5. b   False. The United Kingdom owns the most real estate in the United States.

See Fisher:
    6. a
    7. c
    8. b   False. The real estate market is not as efficient.

See McMillan:
    9. a
    10. b   False. Both statistics are based on variance of expected returns.

See Oliver:
    11. c

See Karnosky:
    12. a
    13. a
    14. a   True.

See Hudson-Wilson:
    15. d
    16. b   False. One should not rely only on historical data.

See Zerbst:
    17. d
    18. a   True.

See Phillips:
    19. c

See Cambon:
    20. b   False.